AF408012

The Open Door Gourmet

Mark Edward Webb

Published by Christina Hamlett, 2024.

While every precaution has been taken in the preparation of this book, the publisher assumes no responsibility for errors or omissions, or for damages resulting from the use of the information contained herein.

THE OPEN DOOR GOURMET

First edition. November 15, 2024.

Copyright © 2024 Mark Edward Webb.

ISBN: 979-8227138118

Written by Mark Edward Webb.

Table of Contents

DEDICATION

There are many people whose encouragement and examples have led me to writing this book. First and foremost is my muse, Christina Hamlett, whose efforts led me to write this book, who appreciates all the meals I have cooked at our dinner table (even the ones that didn't work!) and who, as my beautiful wife, has made all of life's journeys delightful.

For cooking I owe so much to Reda Bellarbi, the owner of Aioli Bodega Espanola in Sacramento California. A place where I have frequented for over 20 years, Reda taught me how to cook outside the box of recipes and of the passion that must be infused in every plating. His friendship is priceless. And thank you as well to his son, Aziz, who will continue this journey for future generations.

Then there is my mother whose cooking skills taught me from an early age that each meal has a purpose. She was also the best pastry cook ever. Growing up I observed, saw, listened and tasted. What remarkable dishes she prepared as part of a culinary journey that worked its way in my family from Virginia to West Virginia to Ohio over the course of 200+ years.

Finally, I have to dedicate this effort to fellow foodies all across the world who respect the honor of the table and what is to be presented to those who are guests. This transcends politics and prejudices, as it should. In every corner of the world there are wonderful people not driven by power or greed but simply to say, "Please, enjoy what I have to offer and let us speak of things that are common amongst us." Would that those in power could accept the grace that is served at tables the world over, without animosity. We could have peace if all were fed...and all that implies.

INTRODUCTION

This isn't a cookbook *per se*. This is a book about cooking and, more specifically, cooking at home. Home cooking is not just comfort food; it is an opportunity to extend your boundaries and gain personal satisfaction from creating a special moment from planning to preparing to plating. With the properly stocked pantry and freezer, gastronomic success can be yours without taking off a day from work. No, this isn't about shortcuts. It is simply a recognition that time does not have to be the biggest barrier to eating well.

This book is about learning how every aspect of a successful meal is interrelated. That starts with understanding why you like the foods you like. Whether it is the soup or appetizer, salad, fish, fowl, meats, starches, vegetables, or dessert, there should be no outliers at the table. As you understand why you like certain foods, planning complementary courses or side dishes becomes much easier. It also allows you to wean yourself off cookbooks—well, sort of.

Cookbooks are invaluable for so many reasons. The cookbooks of today are cultural guides that just happen to have recipes. Putting the flavors of a nation or region into their social context enhances the process of creating a meal. But your goal is to use cookbooks as idea books, not simply a place where you can find a recipe you attempt to execute in strict adherence to the measurements and ingredients you see on the page.

There are downsides to cookbooks. If creating a meal for two people, it is sometimes difficult to understand the appropriate scale when the recipe you are looking to emulate says it will serve eight.

Likewise, not all ovens and stovetops are created equally. You know the tolerances of your own appliances better than the editors of a cookbook. This is a particularly important consideration when you are cooking anything indoors over high heat. It is not a successful meal if at some point in the preparation the smoke alarm goes off. This is especially a consideration when sautéing over high heat using butter or olive oil.

And then there are the subtle and not so subtle issues with substitutions. Many cookbooks today will offer suggestions on how to substitute hard-to-find herbs and spices. They will also provide alternative measurements for dried herbs as opposed to fresh ones. Dried herbs certainly cut down on preparation time and, in many cases, will be an appropriate substitute for fresh herbs. For some dishes, however, the need for fresh herbs is critical. For example, if you are making a *pico de gallo*—a form of fresh salsa using chopped tomatoes, cilantro, onions, chili peppers, and lime juice (among other possible ingredients)—dried cilantro simply will not work. On the other hand, dried oregano, garlic powder, and dried basil are regularly applied seasonings in Italian sauces. Parsley can be very functional both fresh and dried depending on the needs of a particular dish.

Spices, on the other hand, tend to be more frequently available in powdered form. While some recipes, especially Indian recipes, will describe how to take spice seeds, toast them, and grind into powders for curries or creating *garam masala* from scratch, these aromatic spice blends are available commercially or can be made getting ground spices and blending them yourself.

One final note on cookbooks. As you hone your craft in the kitchen, you will learn how much time it takes, and at what temperature, to create your culinary masterpiece. If using a recipe from a cookbook, never assume that the cooking times, temperatures, and amount of liquid in a recipe will work in your oven or on your stovetop. The authors of these wonderful guidebooks, usually, have never been in your kitchen and haven't fixed as much as scrambled eggs for breakfast there.

Trust Your Instincts

Once you take the leap of faith, let your nose be your guide. For those who lunch or dine out regularly, inspiration can come from something as simple as a menu. Imagine you are going to your favorite restaurant for a romantic dinner. It's a Friday night, and you and your spouse are looking forward to a relaxing evening with good food, good wine, and the pressures of the work week fading quickly away. The server brings you a leather-bound menu and you open it. Here's what the menu says: Starters, Salads, Soups, Seafood, Beef, Chicken, Dessert.

That's it.

It would be difficult to trust your palate, let alone the entire meal, to a menu which didn't describe what was being served with sufficient detail to give you a sense of whether you wanted to order a particular dish. But in that menu exists an opportunity to sharpen your cooking skills. When we look at a menu, we gravitate to an offering which causes us to say, "That sounds good". While great food appeals to many senses, usually "sound" is not the first one. How often do you look across the table during a particularly excellent main course and say, "I really like the way this meal sounds." Hopefully not often! Unless you eat a lot of potato chips when you go out. What you do know is that the taste, smell, texture, temperature, and color of the meal appeal to your senses and meet or exceed your expectations.

Why is that? The answer is right there on the menu. Consider the menu of a popular San Francisco seafood restaurant. It doesn't say "fish" and leave you guessing what might be brought to your table. Offering a classic Shrimp Scampi, you know the sauce is made of white wine, garlic, Roma tomatoes, and lemon. How do you know that? Well, because it says so right on the menu. For their ahi, they let you know it is seared rare and encrusted in Cajun spices.

If you order the Scampi and you love it, then ask yourself why does it taste so good? The answer is asking your palate to deconstruct the meal for you. How tart was the lemon, how firm were the tomatoes, why was there just the right amount of garlic? And don't forget the Scampi. Too many? Too few? Were they too large? Too small? Was the linguini on which it was served cooked to the right consistency and was the meal easy to navigate with your utensils?

No matter what the dish, the menu description allows you to think through how each ingredient adds to the flavor and success of the meal. This also makes it easier to understand how a recipe you may try at home can produce the results you seek. So, the next time you go to a restaurant—*any* restaurant—take your thinking cap with you. And when you see a dish with an unfamiliar sauce, don't be shy about asking what is in it. A great meal, regardless of where it is served, is the sum of its parts. Learning how the parts interact can sometimes be as easy as looking a little closer at the menu.

The point here is that a great meal is not a slave to a recipe any more than hard-working people should be slaves to the kitchen. What follows is a collection of original recipes, admitted shortcuts, and useful hints for people who do not have the time to run a gourmet kitchen seven days a week. The recipes are scalable upward, which reflects my own bias against recipes that require too much math to scale downward to two, three, or four people. Cooking does not have to be complicated to be good. Take the time to understand how each part of a recipe has a purpose, from the basic ingredients to the cooking method and temperature. And do not be daunted by making mistakes. There is no such thing as risk-free cooking, unless you make all your meals in a microwave.

As my theatrically savvy beloved also recommends, if you are trying a dish for the first time, have a dress rehearsal before you subject your creation to actual guests. Especially in instances where you can adjust the variance on "heat," it's helpful to know in advance what it's going to taste like and where additions or subtractions will be called for.

Be Careful

Speaking of risk, many people do not appreciate the risk of hosting family and friends at home for a sit-down dinner. As noted in several parts of this book, paying attention to potential allergies is very important, especially with nut or shellfish allergies. Many dishes throughout the world use nuts, and there are also prepared sauces that have nuts in them. Always make certain your guests have no allergies to what you are cooking. This extends to desserts, where people may have sensitivities to fresh fruit as well as nuts.

Also, when hosting or even making a meal for your immediate family, it is required you know exactly what you are serving. There can be "no surprises" when fixing a meal if you are the chef. This is especially the case with chili peppers, using salt, portion control, and how one course interacts with another.

When cooking for others at home also remember that *your* favorite dish may not be *their* favorite dish. It may seem to be a bit of a stretch, but often when we cook for others at home my wife and I ask our guests, "What country would you like to eat from?" From there, we put a menu together for their review. The point of having guests over is to enjoy their company and share the bonds which are reaffirmed over smart conversation while enjoying a fine meal. Having a meal that doesn't work for everyone at the table really means it doesn't work for anyone. So as part of your planning, make certain your guests are part of the process.

While it goes without mentioning, if you are preparing a culinary adventure, including free-flowing wines, which doesn't epitomize the phrase "everything in moderation," plan to serve your guests breakfast the next morning.

One last note. Most of my cooking is pan frying or sautéing. And almost all is with extra virgin olive oil. Olive oils are remarkably diverse in their body and fragrance. I tend to prefer Spanish and Portuguese olive oils, but certainly there are remarkable offerings from Italy, Greece, Sicily and even California. Notwithstanding what you read in some cookbooks, I do not like to cook at high temperatures, which allows for the frequent use of extra virgin olive oil. Regular olive oil (not designated as "extra virgin") has a higher smoke point and can used for higher temperature cooking.

I love to make *patatas bravas*, usually considered a Spanish *tapa*, using extra virgin olive oil that is just hot enough to bubble vigorously when the cubes of potatoes are added. You may wonder whether this longer, lower temperature cooking infuses the potatoes with too much oil. It doesn't, although par boiling the whole potatoes for 10 minutes before frying helps reduce the cooking time. Frying at lower temperatures also means the chance of getting splattered with hot oil is much lower. The bottom line for extra virgin olive oil is that if you use it to pan-fry or sauté, I recommend keeping the oil below its smoke point at all times through the cooking process. As the oil begins to shimmer, place a small drop of batter or even a small piece of bread into the oil and see what happens.

Of course, there are oils which accommodate high heat far better than olive oil. Stir-frying, deep frying, shallow frying, or flash frying dishes require an oil which can withstand high heat for quick cooking. Peanut oil, for example, is often used for stir-fry. There are also recipes that call for "neutral" oils (most often grapeseed or canola oil) that have little if any flavor to them and are also used for high heat cooking. Olive oil, regardless of where it is from, is not a neutral oil.

There is a big difference between cooking oils and oils meant to be used as condiments. On the one hand, there are infused oils which can easily be used for cooking and add a subtle flavor that should be consistent with the overall theme of the meal. Some oils, however, are meant to be used either for dipping or as a finishing flourish to a dish. Toasted sesame oil can be added in small portions to a stir-fry to flavor the high heat neutral oil (or peanut oil) you are using but should not be substituted for the high heat oil appropriate for cooking the meal. Toasted sesame oil, including chili-infused sesame oil, has a wide range of uses from salad dressings to dipping sauces. When buying sesame oil, read the label carefully. Some will even say they are "flavoring oils" on the label. If you have a recipe that simply says, "sesame oil" and the oil is to be used for cooking, then use "pure" or light sesame oil. It has a higher smoke point and is not as strongly flavored as toasted sesame oil.

Lastly, no discussion of frying would be complete without a mention of butter. I like to add butter to the oil for certain dishes I am pan-frying. I think it adds flavor to the dish. Adding butter, however, is not an excuse to cook at a higher temperature. Many dishes use clarified butter or its Indian counterpart, *ghee*. Clarified butter has a higher smoke point than plain butter. News you can use.

So What Does My Book Title Mean?

As I began assembling the recipes I wanted to include, I looked for some sort of unifying theme. Well meaning friends recommended I use my own name in the title. Flattering as this was, Christina and I agreed it would be rather silly. Outside of people we know, strangers would probably scratch their heads and say, "Who is this Mark Webb guy and why should we pay any attention to what he knows about putting meals together?"

Ultimately, my premise reflects the way I have always approached cooking and entertaining. When you come home from work or you are staring down a long weekend and have no idea what you want to eat, there should be enough inspiration in your pantry, fridge and freezer to allow you to put together a meal from anywhere in the world. Even if your culinary ambitions are more pedestrian, you shouldn't be caught late at night—and far from a grocery store—to discover the ingredient most essential to your recipe is something you allowed yourself to run out of.

Instead of being daunted by your own kitchen, you should be able to walk through its open door, put on a smile of confidence and anticipation, and know that everything you need to hone your skills as a gourmet chef is easily within reach.

Mark Edward Webb
Author

This Book Was Nearly Lost

Long before we moved to our forever home at Dobbs Mill, Mark started working on his cookbook. We were living in Pasadena, and I have to say that any guest who ever spent an evening in our dining room urged him to share his amazing recipes.

The only time my talented husband stuck to actual measurements was when he was preparing something new from a cookbook or from *Food & Wine, Gourmet, Bon Appétit*, etc. The rest of the time, his culinary vocabulary consisted of "smidges," "dollops," "tads," "dashes" and pinches." Although I'm sure he wasn't alone in this obscure method of figuring out the allocation of ingredients for an original creation, I emphasized this just wouldn't cut muster if he was ever aiming for publication.

Grudgingly, he began documenting what he was doing. Now and again, he'd print out a few pages to see if he was going in the right direction. To inspire him further, I designed the cover art for him.

The challenges of running his own consulting business and then preparing for our move to a different state, however, left him with less and less time to devote to penning his cookbook. After a while, I stopped asking how it was coming because I realized I was sounding like a little kid who keeps asking, "Are we there yet????"

In late January of 2023, a trip to a specialist revealed he had Stage 4 esophageal and stomach cancer. Absolutely no warning whatsoever this was even in the works, having demonstrated no symptoms during the previous holiday season. His oncologist immediately put him on an aggressive radiation and chemo regimen in the hopes it could put him in remission. Sadly, the cancer had progressed to the point that nothing could be done. By Easter Sunday, he was gone from Lucy and me, dying peacefully in his sleep.

It was during the summer of 2024 that I began wondering what had happened to his notes and recipes. I fervently hoped he hadn't stored them in The Cloud, which completely mystifies me. In taking over our finances and such, I thought I had sussed out where everything was on his various flash drives and the hard drive of his office computer. It was only by a fluke—and a sticky desk drawer—that I accidentally dislodged a little blue flash drive I had previously overlooked. To my delight, it contained the work he had done thus far, as well as his table of contents and the cover art I'd designed for him. Much of my own editorial work on this project involved not only deciphering what his annotations meant but also replicating the dishes myself for accuracy. I think he'd be pleased with the finished product.

As a mirthful sidebar, his amusing promise to haunt me much like Alan Rickman's portrayal of Jamie in *Truly, Madly, Deeply* has manifested in futzing with the thermostat, playing with the lights on the dining room fairy tree, and moving the Turkish rug in my home office. Once I began working on his cookbook, I discovered that the Turkish rug was inexplicably staying in place. Perhaps Mark's message to me was to "get moving" on something. Who knew that he was referring to his work-in-progress?

Can't wait to see what new hauntings the hugsman cooks up to keep me entertained...

Christina Hamlett
Editor

THE KEY TO BEING WELL PROVISIONED

While every family's pantry is going to be different based on their food preferences, dietary restrictions and the size of their kitchen, keeping a variety of ingredients in stock will save you time, money and the panic of last-minute trips to the supermarket.

SPICES
Basil
Black pepper
Bouillion cubes (chicken and beef)
Chili powder
Chinese five spice
Chives
Cilantro
Cinnamon
Coriander
Cumin
Curry powder
Dill
Mustard
Garlic powder
Garlic salt
Ginger
Italian seasoning
Marjoram
Mint

Nutmeg
Onion powder
Onion salt
Paprika
Parsley
Red chili flakes
Rosemary
Saffron
Sage
Salt
Tarragon
Thyme
Turmeric
Vanilla extract
Worcestershire sauce

STAPLES

Apple cider vinegar
Baker's chocolate
Baking powder
Baking soda
Barbecue sauce
Breadcrumbs (Italian seasoned or plain)
Chocolate chips
Chinese mustard
Cocoa powder
Cornmeal
Cornstarch
Crackers (Ritz)
Flour
Honey
Ketchup
Lemon juice (bottled)

Marinades (Indian, Chinese, Thai)
Mayonnaise
Mirin (rice wine)
Non-stick cooking spray
Nuts (cashews, almonds, walnuts)
Oatmeal
Olive oil
Pancake mix
Peanut butter
Salad dressings (ranch, bleu cheese, Caesar, honey mustard, vinaigrette)
Soy sauce
Sugar (brown, granulated)
Sweet chili sauce
Tartar sauce
Vegetable oil
Vinegar
CANNED/PACKAGED
Anchovy paste
Beans (kidney, garbanzos, black beans)
Broth (chicken, beef and vegetable)
Cake mixes
Canned artichoke hearts
Canned fruit
Canned mushrooms
Canned soups
Canned tomatoes, paste and sauce
Canned tuna and salmon
Cereals
Dried soup mixes
Gelatin (plain and flavored)
Gravy packages (brown, mushroom, Hollandaise, turkey)

Instant potatoes
Milk (evaporated, sweetened condensed)
Olives
Pastas (spaghetti, angel hair, elbow macaroni, lasagna, manicotti)
Rice (white, brown, jasmine, herbed, Spanish)
Salsa
Scone and quick bread mixes
Spaghetti sauce
Stuffing
Wasabi

THE FRIDGE

Apple juice
Butter
Carrots
Cheese
Eggs
Heavy whipping cream
Milk
Onions
Orange juice
Russet potatoes
Sour cream

Fresh vegetables and fruit, of course, will have to be purchased as you need them.

THE FREEZER

Chicken (breasts, tenders, thighs, drumsticks)
Frozen vegetables
Ground beef
Ice cream
Microwave meals (for when you just don't feel like cooking at all!)

Pastry dough
Pork chops
Pork tenderloin
Seafood
Steaks
Stew meat

CHEF'S ESSENTIALS

Christina says she wishes a list like this had existed when, as a young struggling actress, she moved into her first studio apartment. Instead, she made copious trips to Macy's on her lunch hour and was directed by motherly kitchen wares staff. They must have directed her well to invest in the good stuff; by the time we got together, she still had most of it.

An excellent set of knives (Do not go cheap on this, buy the best from the get-go)
3 frying pans (small, medium and large)
2 saucepans (1 small, 1 medium)
A wok
2 sheet pans for baking
9-inch ceramic pie plate
Broiler pan (in case your oven doesn't already come with one)
3 mixing bowls (small, medium and large)
Casserole dish
Ladle
Measuring cups and spoons
Oven mitts and potholders
A large pot for pasta
Colander
Funnel
Rolling pin
Tongs, spatulas and flippers
Muffin tins

A large cutting board (plastic or silicon, not wood)
Spoons for stirring (plastic or silicon, not wood)
Small and large whisks
Blender, hand mixer
Grater
Toaster
Electric griddle
Microwaveable plates and bowls
Dish towels

APPETIZERS

When it comes time for entertaining, there is always a place for passed appetizers—some tasty morsel easily navigated by a guest with a drink in one hand and served from a tray passed among the party-goers. But that doesn't mean everything which can be served from a plate is well-suited for your guests. Consider a few simple rules when planning a meal that has passed appetizers and the evening will be an even greater success.

The first is that size matters. That meatball you may enjoy with a sit-down dinner of spaghetti may not be the best thing to ask someone to negotiate while milling about with other guests. A passed appetizer must be easy to eat and preferably in one bite. The same rule applies to rolled appetizers (such as spring rolls) and appetizers served on toast points or crackers.

The second is that hot appetizers need to be warm, not molten. I love Arancini, for instance. These rice balls, often stuffed with cheese, are a wonderful appetizer. That is, wonderful if not too large and not too hot. There is nothing that says "Next stop, dry cleaners" better than a golf-ball sized deep fried ball of breaded rice and cheese which is too big to eat in one bite and served at a temperature that does damage to the roof of your guest's mouth. And it only gets worse if you decide that a nice dip in marinara sauce would be a welcomed addition. It does make the stain more colorful but that may not be your objective.

The third is know your guests and know what you are serving. Any passed appetizer that has in it something which someone may be allergic to should be avoided. If you are doing a satay (peanut sauce) make sure the servers give warnings. The same holds true for shellfish, such as a mini-crab cake, where the allergy-causing food is not obvious to the guests. A colleague of mine once held a church reception at her home. She did the obligatory crudité platter with a host of vegetables. While at the store, she saw some cute little round orange peppers. Unfortunately, she did not know that a habañero is one of the hottest peppers in existence. One of her guests, however, found out the hard way.

Finally, if the appetizers are the only food at the event, then by all means have a diverse, easy-to-eat selection including fruits and vegetables. But if you are having a sit-down dinner as well, plan carefully. How many times have you been at an event where the appetizers were exceptional but by the time you sat down for dinner you were full? While it is not necessary to have a culinary theme with appetizers and dinner following, it *is* important to avoid conflict. The appetizers are the entrée to the main course, so when planning do your best to make the evening a seamless and successful one for hosts and guests alike.

BACON-WRAPPED SCALLOPS

These can be an elegant appetizer or a main course.

Serves 4

Ingredients

16 large sea scallops

8 slices of bacon cut in half

2 tbsp olive oil

¼ tsp salt

¼ tsp pepper

16 toothpicks to secure your creations!

Preparation

Line a large baking sheet with parchment paper. Preheat oven to 425 degrees.

Pat the scallops dry and wrap each one in half a slice of bacon. Secure with toothpicks.

Drizzle olive oil over the scallops and lightly sprinkle the salt and pepper.

Set out the scallops on the parchment paper, allowing ample space between each one.

Bake in the oven for 12-15 minutes and serve immediately.

CHAR-SIU (CHINESE BBQ PORK)

Not long after Christina and I got married, I discovered one of her favorite appetizers at Chinese restaurants was the thinly sliced char-siu. I, thus, made it a quest to replicate the recipe so she could have it whenever she wanted.

Serves 4

Ingredients

1 boneless 2 lb pork tenderloin

1 cup soy sauce

1 cup honey

½ cup dry sherry or sake

4 tbsp crushed garlic

1/3 cup brown sugar

1/3 cup ketchup

1/3 cup hoisin sauce

1 tsp Chinese 5 spice

¼ tsp pepper

¼ tsp salt

¼ tsp cayenne pepper

Red food coloring

Preparation

With the exception of the pork tenderloin and red food coloring, put all of the ingredients in a sauce pan and bring to a boil. Reduce the heat to medium for an additional minute. Remove from stove and allow to cool.

Slice the tenderloin into 3-4 sections.

Thoroughly coat the pork tenderloin pieces with this mixture (along with a few drops of red food coloring), wrap tightly in plastic wrap and refrigerate for 6-12 hours.

Preheat oven to 350 degrees. Line a baking sheet with aluminum foil and place a short cooling rack on top. Place the pork pieces on the rack and heat for 20 minutes. Flip the pork pieces, baste with the remaining marinade and cook for an additional 20 minutes. Messy, yes, but it will smell and taste fabulous!

Allow the pork to cool before slicing thin.

CHEESY CHEDDAR STRAWS

An easy to make and easy to transport appetizer. Hard to say how many it serves since guests will be helping themselves to multiple munchies.

Ingredients

1 lb sharp cheddar cheese (shredded)

1½ cups softened butter

4 cups flour

2 tsp red pepper flakes

1 tsp smoked paprika

1 tsp garlic powder

1 tsp salt

Preparation

Mix everything except the flour in a blender until thoroughly mixed.

Add the flour and mix that in as well.

Use a cookie press with a star-shaped insert to crank out 2-inch ribbons of cheddar dough.

Line a large baking sheet with parchment paper and place the cheddar ribbons in a single layer.

Bake for 12-14 minutes at 350 degrees.

CRAB CAKES

Serves 2

Ingredients

½ cup mayonnaise

1 large egg, beaten

1 tbsp Dijon Mustard

1 tbsp Worcestershire Sauce

1 tbsp Tabasco or other hot sauce

1 tbsp seafood or chowder herb/spice blend

2 tbsp olive oil

½ pound (8 oz.) crab meat

⅔ cup Panko crumbs

Preparation

Mix all the ingredients *except the crab and panko crumbs.*

In a separate bowl, toss the crab meat and the crumbs.

Gently fold the mayonnaise mixture into the crab mixture.

Take mixture and form into patties. Sauté in heated olive oil (or any other oil) for about 3 minutes per side. (I usually use the flipper to press down on the cake while it is cooking to keep the shape). The oil should be not hotter than medium so that the cakes can cook all the way through.

Note: The original recipe I developed uses 1 pound of crab meat to make 8 cakes. That seemed to me, however, to be a little too much crab, which then makes it harder to flip and keep together. This also means these are fairly small crab cakes. In the seafood sections of most supermarkets you can find 8 oz. containers of crab meat which has already been cleaned and picked over.

Alternative: When my lovely wife makes crab cakes, she prefers to purchase small packages of flaked imitation crab. This tastes just like the real deal and is actually a smidge firmer consistency.

FLAWLESS FONDUE

Definitely a sit-down appetizer!

Serves 4

Ingredients

3 cups shredded Cheddar cheese

3 cups Fontina or Gruyere cheese

2 cups whole milk

1 tbsp crushed garlic

3 tbsp flour

3 tsp dry mustard

1 cup dry white wine

Cubed sourdough bread.

Preparation

In a medium saucepan on low, mix together all of the ingredients except the cheeses.

Introduce the Cheddar and Fontina and continue stirring until all of the cheese has nicely melted.

Transfer to your fondue pot. Serve with the cubed sourdough bread.

HOT CRAB DIP

Serves 4

Ingredients

16 oz imitation crab, flaked

8 oz cream cheese, softened

½ cup sour cream

½ cup mayonnaise

½ cup chopped green onion

1 cup grated Gruyere

1 tsp garlic powder

½ tsp red pepper flakes

½ tsp tabasco

Preparation

Preheat oven to 350 degrees.

Thoroughly mix all of the ingredients.

Pour into a casserole dish and bake for 25 minutes.

Serve with crackers or thin sourdough slices.

MUSHROOMS SAUTÉED IN RUBY PORT

This one can also be a side dish.

Serves 4

Ingredients

1 lb small white mushrooms, sans stems

3 tbsp butter

¼ cup olive oil

½ cup ruby port

3 shallots, finely minced

Preparation

Melt the butter and olive oil in a medium saucepan.

Introduce the minced shallots and sauté for 2-3 minutes. (This will be wonderfully aromatic!)

Add the mushrooms to the saucepan and continue to sauté for 5-6 minutes.

Remove the saucepan from the heat and add the port.

Return the saucepan to the stove for an additional 5 minutes of simmering on low.

PALATE PLEASING PINWHEELS

1 tortilla equals 1 serving. Multiply, depending on the number of guests you have.

Ingredients

1 large flour tortilla

1 container commercial red pepper hummus

Thinly sliced roast beef from the deli

Preparation

Microwave the tortilla for 15-20 seconds.

While still warm, smear approximately 2 tbsp hummus over the entire surface.

Add a single layer of thinly sliced roast beef.

Tightly roll the tortilla from one end to the other.

Using a sharp knife, slice into 1" segments.

Variations: Any soft cheese (including cream cheese) can be used as a spread for the base. The next layer can be thinly sliced ham or smoked turkey. Even a non-chunky salsa will work. Use your best

judgment. Anything that is too thick, however, will impede the rolling and slicing.

SALSA FRESCA (PICO DE GALLO)

Serves 4

Ingredients

3-4 Roma tomatoes, firm, chopped

1 cup chopped onions

¼ cup finely chopped cilantro

2 Jalapeño peppers, seeded, cored, and chopped

1 tbsp olive oil

1 tsp garlic power

1 tsp crushed dried oregano

Juice of ½ lime

Pinch of salt

Preparation

Prepare and combine all ingredients. Place in a glass container and let chill for 1 hour or more.

When serving, stir first.

Serve with tortilla chips

The ingredients are somewhat left to the creativity of the person preparing the salsa. If you want something hotter, use Serrano peppers or do not seed and core the Jalapeño peppers. Be very careful about coming into contact with the peppers. Preferably use gloves to avoid getting oils on the hands or in the eyes.

Pico de Gallo can be used in numerous traditional dishes such as carnitas, various tacos, or as part of a queso fundido, a baked cheese appetizer that can also contain meat or vegetables. It can be combined with cooked corn as a side dish to roasted or grilled meats or seafoods or added to black beans. Serrano peppers can be substituted for the jalapeños, or of you want the *Pico* to be *enchiloso* (hot), chop the peppers with the core and seeds in a food processor and add to the mix. It will be much hotter.

SASSY ARANCINI

This is a great meatball-sized Italian hors d'oeuvre which can be made in advance of your dinner and then simply heated up in hot oil. This does, however, come with a warning. If it's a party with passed appetizers and you don't supply small plates for your guests, watch out! Not only is the exterior of the arancini hot but the melty-ness of the inside is even hotter. Christina and I once attended a fundraiser in the Napa Valley where arancini was served in the outdoor courtyard. More than a few guests ended up with arancini falling on the top of their shoes.

Serves 10

Ingredients

1 cup Arborio rice

1 cup finely chopped yellow onion

1 cup grated Parmesan cheese

1 cup Italian breadcrumbs

½ cup finely chopped ham or prosciutto

2 eggs

3 cup chicken stock

8 oz Mozzarella cheese (cubed)

1 tbsp olive oil

Additional oil for frying

Preparation

Heat the 1 tbsp olive oil in a large frying pan. Add the onion and sauté for 2 minutes.

Add the rice and ham/prosciutto and sauté for an additional minute before adding ½ cup of the chicken stock. The rice will absorb rather quickly while you are stirring.

Slowly continue to add the remainder of the chicken stock. The creamy risotto you have created will be done after about 15 minutes. Pour this into a bowl and allow it to cool down in the fridge.

Place parchment paper on the surface of a large baking dish. After your risotto has sufficiently cooled so that you can comfortably handle it, add the eggs and the Parmesan and mix thoroughly. Take 2 tbsp of risotto at a time and form small balls. Press a tsp of mozzarella into the center of each ball and roll to close. Assemble the arancini balls in single rows atop the parchment paper while you heat the frying oil on high in a skillet.

Spread the Italian breadcrumbs on a plate or cutting board and roll each of the arancini balls in it to totally coat. Fry the arancini balls for about 2 minutes or until browned. Serve immediately.

BREAKFAST

Prior to our wedding at Stirling Castle in Scotland, the two of us decided we should combine our households. I give Christina credit for doing most of the heavy lifting and accommodation on this one. I myself brought very little to the domestic equation as the result of a very greedy ex-wife who felt she was entitled to keep everything.

I let her.

Why?

Because I had Christina and she was the world to me.

Still, I wanted to demonstrate that my fiancée's faith in me was justified and this required me to prove I was useful. She knew I enjoyed cooking and, thus, both literally and figuratively gave me the keys to her kitchen and the pantry.

From one of our early conversations, I knew she was a breakfast girl and that she was suspicious of anyone who eschewed the most important meal of the day and only scarfed down coffee on the run. Breakfast, she says, can set the entire tone for how one's day will transpire. (My own regimen B.C.—Before Christina—was usually an apple fritter I noshed on during my commute.)

As news of our culinary capers began to spread among friends, they were immediately struck by how much effort and thought we respectively put into our tablescaping. Not just the plethora of plates and stemware but also the placemats, linen napkins and napkin rings.

"So how do you eat when it's just the two of you?" one of them asked.

"Pretty much the same way we eat when we have guests," I replied, for it was Christina who taught me early on that every meal together was a gift and an occasion to be celebrated.

But I digress...

The first workday morning of our new cohabitation, I decided to surprise her with a three-egg omelet. Though I have since learned that a three-egg omelet can be cut in half for two, my omelet that Monday filled an entire plate and was accompanied by roasted potatoes and bacon.

"Goodness!" she exclaimed when she saw it.

When I told her I wanted to fix something that would get her through the day, the first question she asked was, "How long, exactly, do you think I'll be gone?"

P.S. After we got together, I never had another apple fritter, even on the occasions she was out of town.

BUTTERMILK WAFFLES

Serves 4

In full disclosure, this recipe actually comes from Christina's Aunt Liz. This dear lady was always an apologist for "the first waffle" never turning out right, despite the fact she'd been making them for 50 years. It was always for the same reason, too—that we'd get caught up in talking and drinking Mimosas and she'd have forgotten to use cooking spray on the waffle iron, thus ending up having to scrape crusty waffle shrapnel off the top and bottom.

The first Sunday I met this exceptional woman and her husband (Uncle Bob), Christina said we should stop off at a store and buy her a bouquet of flowers. As Fate would have it, Christina handed me the flowers to hold as I was helping her out of the car. Aunt Liz emerged from the house at that moment, saw the beautiful blooms and proclaimed, "Oh my, what a thoughtful young man you are!" She was just so effusive, I didn't have the heart to tell her whose idea it had been.

Ingredients

¾ cup all-purpose flour

¼ cup cornmeal

1 tsp baking soda

2 tsp baking powder

1 tsp salt

2 eggs, separated

⅓ cup oil

1½ cups buttermilk

Non-stick cooking spray

Preparation

Sift the dry ingredients together. Add the egg yolks to the flour mixture along with the oil and buttermilk.

Beat egg whites until stiff but not dry and fold them into the waffle mixture.

Use non-stick cooking spray on the top and bottom surfaces of your waffle iron. Seriously. Do *not* forget to do this. Spoon a generous amount of waffle batter onto the center of the waffle iron and close the lid. It will steam as it starts cooking. When the light on the waffle iron goes off, your waffle is done and it's time to make the next one.

CHERRY AND WHITE CHOCOLATE SCONES

Serves 8

Ingredients

2 cups self-rising flour

½ cup granulated sugar

½ cup unsalted butter – chilled

½ cup heavy cream

1 egg

2 tsp vanilla extract

½ cup white chocolate chips

1 cup dehydrated dark sweet cherries

½ cup orange liqueur to rehydrate cherries

Preparation

Preheat oven to 375 degrees. Chop cherries at least in half. Dust in a pinch of sugar and then soak in an orange liqueur (Grand Marnier, for example).

Mix flour and sugar. Dice up butter and add to sugar. Using a pastry cutter, mix the butter into flour/sugar mix until it looks like crumbs. Mix egg, cream, and vanilla together and add to flour mixture. Add chips and cherries. With floured hands, place the dough on an ungreased baking sheet and pat into a 9-inch circle. Using a knife, cut into 8 wedges

Bake for 15-18 minutes. Tops should be lightly browned. Cool for at least 5 minutes. Recut wedges if necessary and serve.

THE AWESOME GRUYERE OMELET

Serves 2

I always fancied myself a pretty savvy omelet-maker for any omelets which involved cheese. It wasn't until I met my wife, though, that I learned a nifty trick to making them come out perfect. Specifically, most recipes you'll find on the subject of cheese omeletosity suggest you pour the beaten eggs into a 9" or 10" frying pan, wait until they start to firm up and then dump all the cheese on top. The problem with this approach is that a fat middle tends to make it harder to successfully flip one side over onto the other and give it a nice, golden taco impression. Likewise, the eggs will have been cooking all that time; once the cheese arrives, it still has to melt in order to catch up.

Christina's secret is to blend half of the grated cheese *into* the eggs before it ever gets into the pan. I also cook my omelets on low-medium rather than medium-high heat to lessen the chance of it burning. A perfect omelet should never be rushed.

Ingredients

3 eggs

2 tbsp heavy whipping cream

1 cup grated Gruyere

1 tbsp garlic powder

2 tsp chopped chives

2 tbsp butter

Preparation

Mix together the eggs, heavy whipping cream, half of the grated Gruyere, garlic powder and 1 tsp. of the chopped chives.

Melt the butter in your frying pan. Use a rubber spatula to ensure the butter is evenly distributed around the bottom of the pan instead of clumping up in just one spot and bubbling away. Pour the egg mixture into the pan.

Now is the time to exercise patience as it starts to cook. Lift the pan handle slightly to "tilt" the pan; this allows the liquid in the center to dribble out to the edges and start to form a slight "lip" around the edges. Repeat this process for all four sides to prevent lopsidedness. Evenly distribute the rest of the grated Gruyere on top; specifically, imagine a line running down the center of the omelet and distribute the grated cheese on either side of it. In other words, avoid the center "seam." Continue to cook on low-medium heat until the cheese has mostly melted.

And yes, it's permissible to take a sneak peek at how the bottom of your omelet is cooking. I use a thin pancake turner/flipper for this because it can slide underneath so easily. If the underneath is a nice golden brown, it's time to flip the omelet in half. This will take some practice (because you need to be quick about it) but the trick is to get enough of the turner/flipper under the one side so you can fold it over. The omelet may try to be balky and flop back open but you are the boss of this. Use the turner/flipper to press down on the top half so the insides will stick to each other. Also use this opportunity to nudge the omelet to the center of the pan so it has nowhere to flop open *to*.

Turn the heat off but allow the omelet to sit in the pan for a minute before dividing it into two pieces. Trust me, it's easier to divide it with your turner/flipper while it's still *in* the pan than trying to remove the entire omelet and cut it on a plate. Sprinkle the rest of the chives on top.

CRUSTLESS SCALLION AND RICOTTA QUICHE

Serves 4

There are purists who believe that all quiches should be baked in a homemade or store-bought pie shell. Christina and I are not such people. She taught me early in our marriage that a crustless quiche can be absolutely divine and I agree with her.

Ingredients

6 eggs

1¼ cups heavy whipping cream

1 cup milk

1 cup Gruyere (grated)

1 cup ricotta

10-12 scallions (finely chopped)

1 cup baby spinach leaves

2 tsp salt

½ tsp freshly chopped thyme

Cooking spray

Preparation

Heat the oven to 325 degrees.

In a large bowl, thoroughly mix the eggs, whipping cream, milk, scallions, salt, Gruyere, ricotta and baby spinach.

Spray a ceramic pie dish and pour the custard mixture into it. Sprinkle the thyme on top.

Bake for 45 minutes until the top crust is a nice golden brown.

Remove from oven and allow to "set" (about 20 minutes) prior to slicing.

DIPPY EGGS WITH SOLDIERS

A quintessentially British breakfast!

Serves 1

Ingredients

2 large eggs

2 slices sourdough bread

A healthy schmear of soft butter

1 pinch of salt

Preparation

Boil a small saucepan of water and gently insert the eggs with a spoon. Cook for 5-6 minutes.

Remove the eggs to a bowl of cold water.

Toast your bread, schmear with the butter and cut into narrow strips.

Using a sharp knife or a spoon, remove the top part of the eggshell and egg white. Sprinkle with salt.

Place the egg upright in an egg cup.

Dip your toast piece "soldiers" into the egg yolk and enjoy.

EPIC BREAKFAST POTATOES

Serves 2

Potatoes are a great side to any egg dish and pair nicely with bacon, sausage or ham. The secret is to cook the potatoes first, then set the pan on a back burner on low until everything else is ready to serve. There is also nothing wrong with Just. Having. Potatoes.

Ingredients

3 small white or Yukon Gold potatoes (scrubbed and diced)

½ cup chopped red onion

1 tbsp garlic powder

1 tbsp red pepper flakes

2 tbsp butter

1 tbsp cooking oil

Preparation

Drizzle the cooking oil in a medium frying pan, add the butter and heat on medium.

Sauté the chopped red onion. As it begins to sizzle, add the potatoes, garlic powder and red pepper flakes. Constantly stir the potatoes until they start to darken and get crispy.

Take a sample bite (but don't burn your tongue). If the softness or crispness is to your satisfaction, you can either plate them and serve immediately or shift the pan to a back burner while you fix the rest of the meal.

FRENCH TOAST

Serves 2

This is a departure from most French Toast recipes which use full slices of sandwich bread. Not only are the small slices of French bread easier to coat but also much easier to flip. (You can even use tongs instead of a spatula.)

Ingredients

10 slices of French (not Sourdough) bread sliced ¾" thick

2 eggs

2 tsp vanilla extract

1 tsp ground cinnamon

½ cup milk

Preparation

Whisk the eggs, milk, vanilla extract and ground cinnamon together in a shallow bowl or pie plate.

Dip the sliced bread into the egg mixture and let absorb 3-4 seconds per side.

Cook on a griddle or lightly greased pan at medium heat until brown on both sides.

Serve with butter and warmed maple syrup.

HUEVOS RANCHEROS FOR TWO

Ingredients

4 large eggs

1 can refried beans (I recommend Rosarita™)

2 large tomatoes, diced

½ cup chopped yellow onion

1 tbsp minced garlic

3 tbsp vegetable oil

1 serrano pepper, seeded and finely chopped

1 tsp salt

1 tsp pepper

2 tbsp sour cream

Avocado slices (optional)

4 corn tortillas (the 6-inch size)

⅓ cup vegetable oil for frying tortillas

Preparation

Prepare the salsa portion first by putting the chopped tomatoes, chopped onion, chopped serrano pepper, garlic, salt and pepper in a food processor and blending. If the salsa is too thick to your liking, add a tablespoon of water at a time until it is a consistency you like.

In a small saucepan, heat the 3 tbsp of olive oil to medium. Add the salsa makings and simmer for 3-5 minutes. Remove from the heat but keep warm.

In a large frying pan, pour the ⅓ cup of olive oil and fry the tortillas on medium 1-2 minutes per side. Use tongs to remove them from the oil and drain on paper towels.

Reduce the heat to medium and crack the four eggs into the pan. You'll want them a tad runny for this dish so they shouldn't cook for more than 2 minutes.

Put the refried beans into a microwave container and heat for about 1 minute.

To assemble your meal, spread the refried beans on each of the tortillas. Next comes the fried egg, followed by the salsa.

Finish things off with a generous dollop of sour cream. Garnish with thin avocado slices.

PANCAKES TO PERFECTION

Yes, you can buy a mix where all you add is water but it's not as if you're making *real* pancakes, are you? Plus I can't stress enough that your syrup needs to be served warm. Restaurants often bring it out cold and it just ruins the entire experience. Christina will also tell you that I do not believe bacon should be served on the same plate with the pancakes and syrup. Just a quirk of mine.

Yield: 10 pancakes

Ingredients

2 cups all-purpose flour

¼ cup white sugar

4 tsp baking powder

1 egg

1⅔ cup whole milk or buttermilk

1 tsp cinnamon

1 tsp vanilla extract

Cooking spray

Preparation

Mix the flour, sugar and baking powder in a large bowl.

Add the milk, egg, vanilla and cinnamon and stir until you get all the lumps out.

Use cooking spray on a large electric griddle and heat to medium.

Using a large spoon, do dollops of batter on the griddle's surface.

When tiny bubbles start to appear on the surface of the pancake, it's time to flip it to the other side.

Keep the finished pancakes warm in the oven (set on low) until you're ready to serve.

Note: If you think your batter is too thick, add more milk. If it's too thin, add a smidge more flour.

SALMON SCRAMBLE

A wonderful variation on scrambled eggs!

Serves 4

Ingredients

8 eggs

4 oz. smoked salmon, chopped

½ cup heavy whipping cream

3 tbsp butter

½ cup chopped yellow onion

½ cup chopped chives

Preparation

In a large bowl, mix the eggs and whipping cream until thoroughly blended. Introduce ¼ cup chives.

Add the smoked salmon and onion.

In a large skillet, heat the butter over medium. Pour in the egg and salmon mixture and stir constantly until the eggs are nicely scrambled.

Plate and garnish with the remaining chives.

An Editorial Postscript by Christina

Speaking of chives, there was a wonderful company that used to sell small containers of dried herbs, the chives being our favorite. As is so often the case, however, when you find something you like, the company stops making it. Rather than resort to the tedium of buying fresh chives, chopping them up and drying them, I went on Amazon and bought a 4 oz bag. When it arrived, Mark asked me how much chives I had actually bought since the bag my purchase arrived in was closer to 2 gallons. Yikes! I rechecked my order but it definitely said 4 oz. Which, of course, got us to thinking that chives per se are made of air and truly don't weigh that much. As much as we like to use chives in our cooking, it was pretty clear it would take us a very long time to even put a dent in it. "The chives," Mark prophesied, "are probably going to outlive us." Ironically, he was half right about that.

SOUFFLE SUPREME

Serves 4

Ingredients

5 large eggs

2 cups whole milk

3 cups finely grated Gruyere

6 tbsp all-purpose flour

3 tbsp chopped fresh chives

½ tsp salt

½ tsp pepper

½ tsp nutmeg

Cooking spray

Preparation

In a large saucepan, melt the butter. Whisk in the flour, milk, salt, pepper and nutmeg. Stir constantly until the mixture comes to a boil and becomes thick. Remove from the stove and allow to cool.

Break all five eggs into a bowl and whisk aggressively. Pour the eggs, grated cheese and chives into the butter mixture you just made.

Preheat oven to 400 degrees.

Spray a deep souffle dish with cooking spray and pour everything into it.

Bake for 35-40 minutes or until the puffy top is a nice golden brown. Serve immediately.

VEGETARIAN FRITTATA

For the record, Christina and I are unapologetic carnivores. We do, however, have friends who are vegetarians and this breakfast dish has always dazzled them.

Serves 4

Ingredients

3 large eggs

3 tbsp heavy whipping cream

4 small white potatoes (scrubbed and diced)

1 diced or thinly sliced zucchini

2 Roma tomatoes (diced)

1 can (4 oz) sliced button mushrooms

¼ cup chopped red onion

1 tbsp minced garlic

¼ cup fresh parsley (chopped)

¾ cup grated Gruyere or Swiss cheese

2 tbsp butter

Non-stick cooking spray

Italian breadcrumbs

Optional: Cayenne

Preparation

Preheat oven to 350 degrees.

In a large bowl, whisk the eggs and cream. Set aside for the moment.

Melt the butter in a large frying pan. Sauté the onion, garlic and vegetables (including the potatoes) on medium heat for 2-3 minutes.

Transfer the vegetables into the bowl with the eggs and cream and blend together.

Add the grated cheese and parsley. Thoroughly mix. If you'd like your frittata to have some zing, add a few dashes of cayenne.

Spray a 9" ceramic or Pyrex pie dish with non-stick cooking spray.

Fold the egg/cheese/veggie mixture into the dish and sprinkle the top with Italian breadcrumbs.

Bake for 20-25 minutes.

Upon removal from the oven, let it set for 2-3 minutes before slicing and serving.

CONDIMENTS, MARINADES AND SAUCES

A colleague once asked, "What do you look for in a good bottle of wine?" My response was simple: "One that tastes good." There is no more magic to everyday food and drink than taste. Of course, elaborate and time-consuming preparations using fresh ingredients will move your guests to praise your culinary skills, but we also live in a world where it is not always easy to take half a day to stage a meal. And therein lies the rub. Literally.

Each pantry should contain the basic dried herbs and spices that can get you around the world in a matter of teaspoons. These are: Basil, Cinnamon, Coriander, Cumin, Dill, Garlic Powder (not salt), Nutmeg, Oregano, Paprika, Red Chili Powder, Rosemary, Sage, Tarragon, Thyme, and Ground White Pepper. Of course, you already have sea salt and black pepper in grinders somewhere on the countertop.

As you shop at your favorite market, you will also note an increasing number of herb and spice blends which can be used for various styles of cooking. Look at the ingredients and you can see how the selective use of herbs and spices give foods their distinctive national or regional flavor. Whether it is a Moroccan Rub (which will have cinnamon), or Herbs de Provence (which includes lavender), these blends can add remarkable flavor in short order to virtually any meal.

Some of the items on the shelf may pique your curiosity and are worth a closer look. Other times, it can be helpful to research online purchases. For example, I buy many blends from The Spice and Tea

Exchange (https://www.spiceandtea.com/). I know what I am buying, usually, because they have sample jars and I can smell the blend. The problem is that the store I shop at is in Alexandria, Virginia (there is also one closer in San Francisco). Still, you can see online what the blends are and what they are made of. One I use is "Sweet Heat," a combination of dried peppers, salt, onion, and tomato powder.

You can take a risk with the purchase, but you don't have to with the meal. Simply put some extra virgin olive oil in a small dish and sprinkle some of your blend into it. A dipped piece of bread is all you need to see if you made a wise purchase. And spice infused olive oils with bits of French bread for dipping make a wonderful appetizer.

A few cautionary notes. Spices and herbs have a cumulative effect. If you are making a highly spiced main dish, don't have a highly spiced sauce over it. You may have a mustard caper sauce down to perfection, but placing it over a roasted pork tenderloin which you have encrusted with a Moroccan rub may have your guests saying, "Well, that was odd..." Also, some spice blends have an inordinate amount of salt in them so be careful. Let your nose and mouth do the lifting and your meal will awe everyone at the table.

A word on salt and pepper is in order. As an example, I enjoy the various salts that are available from Hawai'i. Most of the time, I use red Hawai'ian sea salt. I do like salts infused with garlic, peppers, truffles, or Herbs de Provence. I have grinders for each salt I use. This tends to result in using less salt, which is also why I never try to measure the salt as it will invariably wind up using more salt than is needed.

I also have grinders for all the peppers I use, whether black, green, Szechuan, or white. I do not grind white peppercorns often, as I find the commercial finely ground powders better for sauces or spice blends, which is where I most often use them. I also look at prepared spice blends closely to see whether they use salt. If they do, I will not add salt to any part of the recipe.

A note on aioli. This will appear in many times and in many forms throughout this book. It is a remarkable condiment, and not just for French and Spanish food. Stonewall Kitchens, for example, makes a wonderful commercial Sriracha Aioli that is exceptional with Asian food or as a *crema* for fusion street tacos. With the proper ingredients, it is also a great substitute for tartar sauce on seafood dishes. For example, consider a Jerk crab cake with a habanero aioli or a Provençal crab cake with a lavender aioli (more on these later). And how can one serve *pomme frites* or *patatas bravas* without the appropriate aioli?

Aioli is basically a garlic mayonnaise. Since I do not do much with raw eggs until they are cooked, if I want to make an aioli I start with commercial mayonnaise and then add the appropriate ingredients. Aioli should not be as thin as a sauce nor as thick as mayonnaise. The proper consistency should either lightly coat what is dipped (frites or asparagus, for example) or rest gently and smoothly on top of what it is placed upon.

As noted, however, if I want to just buy an aioli, I will look to the Spanish purveyor Matiz—hard to find commercially but available at Whole Foods and online, or the aiolis from Stonewall Kitchen, generally more available. There are flavored aiolis on the market that may also prove a good addition in the appropriate circumstance.

MY FAVORITE SPICE PURVEYORS

Just to get you started on your own spice journey:
 Aloha Spice Company (http://alohaspice.com/)
 Amigo Foods (https://www.amigofoods.com/)
 Delicias de España (http://www.tiendadelicias.com/)
 La Tienda (https://www.tienda.com/)
 My Spice Sage (https://www.myspicesage.com/)
 Peppers.com (http://www.peppers.com/)
 Savory Spice (https://www.savoryspiceshop.com/)
 Smith & Truslow (https://smithandtruslow.com/)
 Spice Tribe (https://www.spicetribe.com/)
 Spices at Penzeys (https://www.penzeys.com/)
 Stonewall Kitchen (http://www.stonewallkitchen.com/)
 The Chile Shop Santa Fe (http://thechileshop.com/)
 The Spice and Tea Exchange (https://www.spiceandtea.com/)
 Urban Accents (https://www.urbanaccents.com/)
 Vanns Spices (https://www.vannsspices.com/)
 Zamouri Spices (https://www.zamourispices.com/)

BÉCHAMEL SAUCE

A cheesy French white sauce which often makes appearance in casseroles, souffles and over fish and fresh vegetables.

Yields about 2 cups of sauce.

Ingredients

2 cups whole milk

6 tbsp butter

4 tbsp flour

Preparation

Lightly warm the milk in the microwave.

Gently melt the butter in a medium saucepan.

Sprinkle in the flour and stir for about 6 minutes.

Add the warmed milk just a few tablespoons at a time.

Stir constantly until the sauce has nicely thickened.

COCKTAIL SAUCE

Yields 1 cup

Ingredients

1 cup ketchup

2 tbsp fresh lemon juice

2 tbsp Worcestershire sauce

2 tbsp creamy horseradish sauce

1 tsp garlic cloves, minced

1 tsp Tabasco sauce

Preparation

Mix all ingredients and store in refrigerator for up to three weeks. Serve chilled.

CRÈME FRAÎCHE

Sure, you can take the easy way and buy this in the grocery store but, given the simplicity, isn't it fun to make it yourself? Just about any recipe which calls for sour cream can be swapped out with crème fraîche.

Yields 1 cup

Ingredients

2 tbsp plain yogurt

1 cup heavy whipping cream

Preparation

Mix the ingredients in a small, lidded bowl and refrigerate overnight prior to use.

HOLLANDAISE SAUCE

Yields 1 cup

If there are Eggs Benedict in your future, it's time you learned how to make the hollandaise which tops it to perfection.

Ingredients

1 stick unsalted, melted butter

3 egg yolks

2 tbsp fresh squeezed lemon juice

1 pinch each of salt and pepper

Preparation

Put the egg yolks in a blender. Add the lemon juice.

While the blender is still running, gently pour in half of the melted butter until a creamy sauce is formed.

Pour this mixture into a bowl and use a whisk to add the remainder of the butter. Sprinkle in the salt and pepper.

HONEY MUSTARD SAUCE

A great choice to drizzle over shrimp, chicken, vegetable and pork dishes.

Yields 1 cup.

Ingredients

¾ cup plain yogurt

2 tbsp Dijon mustard

¼ cup honey

¼ tsp salt

Preparation

Mix all of the ingredients in a lidded bowl until smooth. Refrigerate for up to a week.

INDIAN PEANUT SAUCE

Yields 1 cup

Ingredients

⅓ cup peanut butter (creamy, not chunky!)

3 tbsp soy sauce or tamari

2 tbsp fresh squeezed lemon juice

2 tbsp rice wine vinegar

1 tbsp siracha

1 tbsp red chili flakes

2 tbsp honey

3 tbsp warm water

Preparation

Thoroughly mix all of the ingredients by hand until creamy. If you'd like your peanut sauce a little thinner, add 1 tbsp of warm water at a time.

INDONESIAN BEEF MARINADE

Yields 1 cup.

Ingredients

½ cup soy sauce

¼ cup kecap manis

3 tbsp rice vinegar

2 tsp garlic, minced

1 tbsp ginger (prepared minced)

2 tbsp sesame oil

½ c. Chinese Rice wine

2 tsp Spice Worcestershire Sauce

2 tsp Sambal Badjak

Preparation

Combine ingredients. Boil and then simmer for 10 minutes. Cool prior to marinating beef.

LEMON BUTTER SAUCE

If you're looking for an easy way to jazz up your fish, chicken, pasta, scallops, vegetables or even a plate of rice, you've come to the right place. This is one of the easier sauces to make, although many of them don't go beyond butter, cornstarch and lemon juice. (Boring!) My own version is creamier and adds just the right amount of tanginess. When done properly, it will have the color and consistency of Hollandaise and, in fact, could be spooned over your morning poached eggs.

Ingredients

4 tbsp unsalted butter

1 cup heavy whipping cream

1 cup white wine (Chardonnay is a good choice)

1 smashed garlic clove

2 tbsp fresh squeezed lemon juice

Salt and pepper

Preparation

Heat the wine and smashed garlic clove in a small saucepan over medium heat. Bring the mixture to a simmer and stir until it is reduced by half.

Pour in the cream and gently whisk until it has reduced.

Add the lemon juice.

Remove saucepan from the heat and add the unsalted butter 1 tbsp at a time.

Add salt and pepper to taste prior to serving.

Note: Make the sauce just before you plan to use it. Attempting to make it ahead and store it in the refrigerator will only cause the ingredients to separate.

MUSHROOM GARLIC SAUCE

This is a nice addition to chicken and pork dishes, makes 2-3 cups and can be kept in the fridge for up to a week.

Ingredients

2 cups heavy whipping cream

1 cup sliced button mushrooms

4 tbsp crushed garlic

2 tbsp olive oil

Salt and pepper to taste

Preparation

In a medium frying pan, heat the olive oil. Sauté the sliced mushrooms in it for 7-8 minutes.

Add the crushed garlic and sauté for an additional minute.

Introduce the heavy whipping cream and keep simmering until the liquid has been reduced by half.

Add salt and pepper to taste.

SAFFRON ORANGE AIOLI

Is there anything better with fish-dishes than a homemade aioli? The saffron and citrus in this one add a lovely taste of the exotic. Yes, saffron is a pricey ingredient but oh so delicious.

Ingredients

1 garlic clove (finely chopped)

¼ tsp saffron threads (crumbled)

1 tsp orange zest

¼ cup fresh orange juice (no pulp)

1 tbsp lemon juice

½ tsp salt

¼ tsp black pepper

¾ cup olive oil

1 egg yolk

Preparation

Dissolve saffron in 1 tbsp of hot water. Put this mixture in a food processor with the garlic, orange zest, orange juice, lemon juice, salt, pepper and egg yolk. Blend on a low pulse.

Slowly add the olive oil last and continue blending until the sauce has thickened.

Transfer to a lidded bowl and keep in refrigerator. This aioli can be made up to a day before you plan to use it.

SPICY THAI MARINADE

This make-ahead marinade is as applicable to beef dishes as it is to chicken and seafood. Makes about a cup of marinade.

Ingredients

8 tbsp minced garlic

2 tbsp fish sauce

2 tbsp Sambal Oelek (Asian chili sauce also works for this)

½ cup vegetable oil

¼ cup finely chopped cilantro

¼ cup finely chopped basil

1 tsp lime zest

1 tsp lemon zest

Preparation

Mix all of the ingredients and store in lidded container in refrigerator until use.

STILTON AND PORT SAUCE

When Chistina and I honeymooned in Edinburgh, Scotland, we came across a wonderful restaurant on The Royal Mile which served filets smothered in a Stilton and tawny port sauce. The restaurant is no longer there, but the delicious memories still linger!

Ingredients

¾ cup Stilton

¾ cup heavy whipping cream

1 shallot, finely chopped

1 tbsp minced garlic

1 tbsp olive oil

3 tbsp tawny port

Preparation

In a small saucepan over medium, heat the olive oil and sauté the shallot and the garlic for 2-3 minutes.

Remove the saucepan from the heat and add the port.

Return the saucepan to the stovetop and introduce the heavy whipping cream, stirring constantly as the mixture thickens.

Crumble the Stilton and sprinkle it into the mixture. Stir until the mixture is smooth and ready to serve. Note: If you feel the sauce is too thick, it's up to you to add more port or more cream.

TANGY RÉMOULADE

Or as a friend of ours nicknamed it "Ray Milland." This dipping sauce is a nice condiment for seafood, fried foods, crab cakes, roasted potatoes and even sandwiches.

Ingredients

½ cup mayonnaise

2 tbsp horseradish

3 tbsp mustard (coarse grained)

2 tbsp scallions (finely cut)

½ tsp lemon juice

½ tsp paprika

½ tsp cayenne pepper

Salt and pepper to taste

Preparation

Whisk together all ingredients in a small lidded bowl and chill in the fridge for up to two days.

Note: The amount of cayenne can go up or down depending on your tolerance for spicy heat.

VINDALOO RUB

If you like something with a little kick, this vindaloo is just the ticket for chicken, lamb, seafood and vegetables.

Ingredients

3 tsp garlic powder

1 tsp powdered ginger

1 tsp hot red chili powder

1 tsp hot green chili powder

1 tsp cumin

1 tsp turmeric

Salt

Pepper

Preparation

Mix all of the ingredients and either rub directly into your meat of choice or introduce liberal sprinkles to stews, noodles, soups, pasta and vegetables.

SOUPS, SALADS, STEWS AND STARCHES

Soups and salads often precede restaurant meals and holiday dinners. Just as with appetizers, though, you don't want to so front-load the menu that your guests are stuffed before the main course even makes it to the table. Likewise, a heavy cream-based soup or a large salad with a rich and creamy dressing will be on a collision course with an entrée smothered in cream sauce!

Soups and stews are great vehicles to experiment with a wide variety of foods. While traditional soups such as chicken noodle, beef vegetable, or clam chowder provide an opportunity to create a hearty meal for a dark and stormy night and still add a dash of individuality, there are also a multitude of "what if?" options that can be either a first course or the main attraction any time of the year. But, before thinking about soups or stews from scratch, take a moment online or with your cookbook collection to look at how soups and stews are as varied as the global cuisines from which they take their cue.

Moving on to starches...

From the simple to the complex, rice can be an integral part of the texture, presentation, and flavor of your main course. It all begins with the prototypical pilaf. The word "pilaf" is derived from Middle Eastern and Indian terms for a seasoned rice dish usually cooked in a meat stock. What aromatic additions you use in the rice and what liquid you cook it in is truly up to you. As is the case with any part of a meal, the rice needs to be compatible with the main course. For example, I would not suggest serving the Spanish version of Arroz Negro with an herb roasted chicken. I might think about it with grilled swordfish, however, because the liquid that gives this rice its deep black color is squid ink.

Generally, long-grain white rice is recommended for a pilaf. This can be plain (milled) white rice, basmati rice, with a slight nutty flavor often used in Indian cooking, or jasmine rice, which as the name suggests is a rice with a floral aroma to it that comes from Thailand.

In the pan in which you are going to cook the rice, sauté some chopped onion (or shallot) in olive oil over medium heat. To that onion you can add several other ingredients, including chopped garlic and seasonings. Depending on the meal this can include regional seasoning blends which will complement the seasonings used on your main course. I would not recommend using the same seasoning as the main course out of concern of too much of a good thing!

The rice is then added to this aromatic mixture and coated in the oil. Once fully coated and slightly toasted, add your liquid. Chicken stock is often used for many pilafs and is complimentary to most types of cooking. Remember that rice generally needs to have a delicate flavor as its role as best supporting side dish, so be careful not to overdo the herbs, spices, and other additions, such as tomatoes, fruit, nuts, or chili peppers, unless called for in the dish you are creating. What works for a North African dish may not work for an Asian or Latin American meal.

While a traditional pilaf uses meat stock, that is not your only option. Various types of teas, from a strong black tea to fruit and herbal blends, can add a subtle flavor to traditional long-grain white rice. Also, turmeric is a wonderful mix to any white rice dish. Not only is it good for you from a nutritional standpoint, but it also brings a bright yellow color to the rice. If you want to be particular impressive with the presentation of a dish – and particularly if you are making Indian food – consider two pans of rice, one with turmeric and one without. Combine them for serving.

There are lots of choices to make when deciding what rice to use. While long-grain white rice is used in many dishes, there are also more robust choices such as brown, red (such as Camargue or Himalayan), black and wild rices that can highlight your meal. These rices tend to be firmer and more flavorful than white rice so your herb, spice, and stock selections should not detract from their natural flavor.

There is also the short-grain Arborio rice used in risotto. Risotto is in a league all its own. It is not just a side dish. Risotto can be a meal unto itself with any wide range of meats, seafood, or vegetables folded in before serving. Like paella, there is a patience required, and great attention needed, to make risotto. It is always well worth the effort.

Directions, quantities, cooking times and many other recommendations can be found in virtually any cookbook or online recipe collection. Experiment and enjoy. When looking at rice recipes, from simple to complex, however, also take note of the cooking times and amount of liquid to be used. Not all instructions work for all stovetops or at all altitudes.

Another starch which deserves consideration is couscous. There are primarily two types of couscous on the market: Israeli couscous, a larger grain, and Moroccan couscous, a small grain. Lebanese couscous is also available and is larger than Israeli couscous. Couscous is a very healthy grain. It can be used as a side dish for any type of meal as a substitute for rice or potatoes. But it should not be looked at as a second thought – couscous is an equal on the table for any meal you are making. Israeli couscous is also used in salads.

And then there are potatoes. There are a few things we eat that can be considered ubiquitous. Potatoes are in that category. Whether boiled, baked, mashed, fried, sliced, diced, roasted or stuffed, potatoes can work their way into virtually any dish from anywhere. Potatoes are also the most innocent of foods. Alone, there is nothing particularly harmful about a potato. Ah, but it is what we *do* to these spuds which causes alarm from health professionals. They are, after all, a remarkable vehicle to transform a basic starch into a dish fit for the most ambitious of gourmands. Butter, cream, cheese (my favorite is grated Gruyère), herbs, grated truffles, or even bacon or lobster have at one time or another found their way into potato dishes.

Potatoes can be a side dish or an integral part of many dishes, such as soups or stews. Roasted baby potatoes are particularly well-suited for roasted meat dishes as they cook alongside a meat or poultry main course in the oven. Properly prepared, they are used as the top crust for a Shepherd's Pie.

ARROZ CON POLLO

Serves 4

Ingredients

12 boneless, skinless chicken thighs

1 large can diced tomatoes

1 cup long-grain rice

1½ cups chicken broth

1 large yellow onion, diced

2 red bell peppers, seeded and cut into strips

4 tbsp minced garlic

3 tbsp olive oil

2 tbsp tomato paste

2 tsp garlic powder

1 tsp cayenne

2 tsp ground cumin

1 tsp dried oregano

½ cup fresh chopped cilantro

¼ tsp salt

¼ tsp pepper

Preparation

Mix the salt, pepper, cayenne, garlic powder, cumin and oregano. Rub this mixture into the chicken thighs.

In a large frying pan, heat the oil to medium and brown the chicken thighs 4-5 minutes on each side. Remove to a separate plate.

Using the same pan, sauté the onion and bell peppers for 4-5 minutes. Introduce the minced garlic and tomato paste, continuing to stir for another minute.

Next, add the rice and continue to stir for 3-4 minutes. This will be followed by the chicken broth and tomato paste.

Bring the chicken thighs back to the frying pan and allow to simmer uncovered for approximately half an hour.

Plate the meal and garnish with the fresh chopped cilantro.

BABY CARROT CREAMY SOUP

Serves 4

Ingredients

2 cups sliced baby carrots

1 large russet potato (peeled and cut into cubes)

½ cup butter

1 cup chopped yellow onion

3 cups chicken broth

½ cup heavy whipping cream

1 tsp curry powder

1 tsp ground ginger

¼ tsp salt

¼ tsp pepper

Crème fraiche

Preparation

Melt the butter in a large, deep saucepan. Add the onion, potato, carrots, ginger and chicken broth. Stir constantly for half an hour until all of your vegetables are tender.

Allow to cool for 15 minutes before transferring to a food processor. Blend until your mixture is creamy. (Note: You can also use a hand blender but it will take you longer and may splatter if you're not careful.)

Return to the large saucepan and fold in the heavy whipping cream, curry powder, salt and pepper.

Heat on low for an additional 10 minutes.

Put into soup bowls and dollop each with crème fraiche.

BABY PEA AND POTATO SOUP

Serves 4

Ingredients

2 medium yellow onions, diced

2 cups baby peas (frozen peas are perfectly acceptable for this)

3 cups russet potatoes (diced)

3 tbsp minced garlic

4 cups beef stock

2 tbsp butter

2 tbsp olive oil

½ tsp salt

½ tsp pepper

Preparation

In a large saucepan, melt the oil and butter on medium and sauté the diced onion for about 10 minutes.

Introduce the potatoes, beef stock, garlic, salt and pepper and bring to a nice boil. Reduce the heat, cover the saucepan and cook for half an hour.

Add the baby peas and simmer uncovered for an additional 10 minutes.

BAKED MAC AND CHEESE

I've been told this is a great recipe but Christina refuses to eat it. Owing to an unfortunate incident in second grade with cafeteria macaroni and cheese—well, who can blame her? What they serve in school cafeterias is out of a box and pretty much equates to prison food.

Serves 4

Ingredients

8 oz commercial pasta (my pref for this is shells because they soak everything up effortlessly)

5 oz sharp Cheddar cheese (shredded)

5 oz Gruyere (shredded)

2 cups whole milk

2 tbsp soft butter

2 tbsp flour

¼ tsp salt

¼ tsp pepper

¼ tsp garlic powder

Cooking spray

Preparation

Cook the pasta al dente.

In a large saucepan, heat the milk, butter and flour and whisk until creamy.

Preheat oven to 400 degrees and spray a baking dish.

Add the cheese and spices to what is in the saucepan and continue to stir.

Drain the pasta and pour into the saucepan with the rest, continuing to stir.

Transfer the mixture to the baking dish.

Bake in the oven for 20-25 minutes or until it starts to get bubbly.

CAJUN RISOTTO

Serves 2

Ingredients

5 strips bacon (finely sliced)

4 oz Andouille sausage (sliced)

½ cup chopped yellow onion

2 cloves crushed garlic

2 Roma tomatoes (diced)

1 cup arborio or paella rice

2 cups chicken stock

1 tbsp olive oil

½ cup grated Parmesan

¼ cup chopped parsley

Preparation

Heat the bacon and sausage over medium. Add onions, garlic and olive oil.

Sauté for 5 minutes. Add tomatoes.

Add chicken stock and heat to boiling.

Cover with rice. Reduce to low and heat for an additional 20 minutes.

Serve and garnish with grated Parmesan and parsley.

CHICKEN SALAD

This can either be eaten as an amusing side dish or spooned into large croissants and served as sandwiches. My fondest memory of the latter is the rainy day Christina and I decided to play hooky. We made the croissant sandwiches, put them on a breakfast tray with two flutes of champagne and sat in bed watching *Victor/Victoria*.

Serves 2

Ingredients

I boneless skinless chicken breast, cubed

1 tbsp. Coastal Blend seasoning from the Spice and Tea Exchange (https://www.spiceandtea.com)

1 tsp extra virgin olive oil

2 tbsp white wine (or mirin)

2 tbsp sliced green onion tops

1 tbsp Dijon mustard

1 cup mayonnaise

½ cup cashews

Croissants

Preparation

Sauté chicken in olive oil until browned. Add white wine and seasoning and bring to a boil. Simmer until most of the liquid is absorbed. Place in a container and let chill overnight.

Next morning, preferably 2 hours before serving, add the remaining ingredients and let chill.

COMFORT BEEF STEW

Serves 4

Ingredients

2 lbs chuck, cut into bite-sized cubes

1 medium yellow onion (diced)

2 tbsp minced garlic

1 tbsp flour

1 bottle (yes, an entire bottle!) of dry red wine

4 slices of uncooked bacon (in one-inch pieces)

1 dozen cremini mushrooms, finely sliced

1 dozen baby carrots, peeled and halved

2 tbsp butter

2 tbsp olive oil

1 tsp salt

1 tsp pepper

Preparation

In a large oven-proof casserole dish, heat 1 tbsp of butter and 1 tbsp of olive oil. Brown the beef cubes on all sides for 8-10 minutes. Add salt and pepper.

Introduce the garlic and onion and continue to stir on medium.

Sprinkle in the flour.

Pour in the entire bottle of wine. Bring to a boil for 3 minutes, continuing to stir.

Preheat the oven to 350 degrees.

Put the lid on the casserole dish and place on the middle rack of the oven. Cook for 1½ hours. Your kitchen will start to smell so wonderful, you may as well open some more wine and pour yourself a glass while the stew is cooking.

In a small saucepan, brown the bacon pieces. Add the remaining butter and olive oil along with the sliced mushrooms and carrots. Simmer for about 15 minutes on low.

When the casserole comes out of the oven, stir in the bacon, mushrooms and carrots.

Serve with crusty sourdough bread. And more wine. Definitely more wine.

COMFORT CORN CHOWDER

Twas a dark and stormy night. It could, of course, also be chilly Autumn afternoon when you're looking for something to warm you from the inside out. Sticky Fingers™ Cheddar and Chive scones are the perfect accompaniment.

Serves 2-4

Ingredients

3 cups chicken stock

6 oz boneless, skinless chicken thighs

3 strips bacon

½ cup chopped onions

1 tsp cumin

2 tbsp ancho chili powder

3 tbsp olive oil

1 package frozen corn

1 small can diced green chiles

2 medium russet potatoes

1 cup milk

1 tbsp butter

Oregano, garlic power and pepper – to taste

Directions

Make the mashed potatoes in advance. The milk and butter you use will make your mashies thin. Set aside.

In a large pan, sauté the chicken with onions and spices in the olive oil on medium heat.

Chop bacon into small pieces and add to the chicken.

Add the chicken stock and simmer for 5-10 minutes.

Add the mashed potatoes, frozen corn and green chiles.

Simmer covered for approximately 20 minutes.

CREAMY SCALLOPED POTATOES

Serves 4

Ingredients

4 cups russet potatoes, peeled and sliced thin

1 cup shredded Cheddar cheese

1 cup yellow onion, chopped

1½ cups whole milk

3 tbsp flour

2 tbsp butter

¼ tsp salt

¼ tsp pepper

Cooking spray

Preparation

Preheat the oven to 375 degrees. Spray the bottom and interior sides of an 8x8 inch baking dish.

In a medium saucepan, melt the butter. Introduce the flour, milk, salt and pepper and stir until thick and smooth. Remove the saucepan from the heat and sprinkle in the shredded cheese.

Place a layer of potatoes in the bottom of the baking dish, followed by a layer of onions and a layer of cheese sauce. Repeat this layering until everything has been used up.

Place a cover or aluminum foil on the baking dish and bake for 50 minutes.

Remove the cover and bake for an additional 10 minutes.

DON'T SKIMP ON THE SHRIMP CHOWDER

Serves 4

Ingredients

1 lb large shrimp, sans shells and tails

4 slices bacon, cut into 1-inch pieces

1 medium yellow onion, chopped

2 cups heavy whipping cream

3 cups chicken broth

1 lb red potatoes, quartered

3 tbsp flour

1 tsp tomato paste

2 tbsp olive oil

¼ tsp salt

¼ tsp pepper

½ cup fresh basil, chopped

Preparation

In a large skillet, brown the bacon pieces over medium heat until crisp. Add the olive oil, chopped onion and tomato paste. Sprinkle with the flour until a nice paste forms.

Introduce the chicken broth and heavy whipping cream and stir until smooth. Add the salt, pepper and red potato quarters. Simmer covered, for about 15 minutes.

Lastly, add the shrimp and cook for about 4-5 minutes.

Garnish with the chopped basil.

ELEGANT ASPARAGUS

A lovely alternative to traditional salad.

Serves 4

Ingredients

2 lbs asparagus (cut off the lower fourth of each spear)

6 tbsp butter

3 tbsp minced garlic

3 tbsp fresh squeezed lemon juice

1 hardboiled egg, nicely chopped

2 tsp fresh tarragon, minced

Preparation

In a medium skillet, melt the butter over medium. Sauté the garlic for a minute. Remove from the heat but keep warm.

Boil the asparagus spears for 5 minutes. Drain and plate.

Stir the egg and lemon juice into the still-warm garlic butter.

Pour the egg and lemon juice mixture over the asparagus.

Sprinkle tarragon on top.

ENGLISH PEA SALAD

Serves 4

Ingredients

For the Dressing:

¾ cup sour cream

1/8 cup mayonnaise

1 tsp sugar

½ tsp salt

¼ tsp black pepper

For the Salad:

3 slices bacon, cooked and crumbled (Note: if you're in a hurry, you can use bacon bits)

1 bag frozen petit pois or baby sweet peas, thawed

½ cup Cheddar cheese (cubed)

¼ cup chopped red onion

2 hard-boiled eggs, chopped

1½ tsp fresh dill, minced

Preparation

Cook the bacon slices, drain, and crumble when cooled.

In a large lidded bowl, mix the sour cream with the mayonnaise, then add the sugar, salt and pepper.

Add the peas, the cubed cheese, the chopped onion and the chopped eggs. Introduce the dill.

Once everything is mixed together, cover and refrigerate until you're ready to serve.

One final note: Allow the salad to come to room temperature for 30 minutes before serving to your guests.

ITALIAN SAUSAGE AND BABY SPINACH SOUP

Serves 4

Ingredients

1 lb ground Italian sausage

1 medium yellow onion (chopped)

32 oz chicken broth

1 large can of undrained garbanzo beans

1 bag baby spinach

2 tbsp olive oil

1 tsp Italian seasoning

¼ tsp salt

¼ tsp pepper

¼ red chili flakes

Preparation

Heat the olive oil in a large saucepan over medium.

Brown the Italian sausage for 10-12 minutes. Remove with a slotted spoon and set aside on a separate plate.

Using the same oil in the pan, sauté the chopped yellow onion, salt, pepper, red chili flakes and Italian seasoning.

After 2-3 minutes, introduce the garbanzo beans and simmer.

Add the sausage to the saucepan, along with the chicken broth and baby spinach. Bring to a simmer and constantly stir for about 10 minutes.

I recommend serving with Sticky Fingers™ Cheddar and Chive scones or sourdough bread. Fireplace optional!

LEMON CHICKEN SOUP WITH ORZO

Serves 4

Ingredients

3 boneless, skinless chicken breasts, cut into bite-size pieces

8 cups chicken stock

2 russet potatoes, peeled and cubed

2 tbsp fresh lemon juice

1 cup shallots (sliced thin)

¾ cup uncooked orzo

2 tbsp olive oil

1 tbsp fresh chopped rosemary

2 tsp salt

¼ cup fresh parsley, chopped

Preparation

Heat the oil in a large cooking pot. Sauté the shallots and rosemary over medium heat.

Add the lemon juice, chicken stock and potatoes and bring to a vigorous boil.

Reduce heat. Add the chicken pieces and salt and cook for 15 minutes on medium. Add the uncooked orzo and cook for an additional 10-15.

Garnish with parsley.

Note: A variation on this recipe is to parboil the chicken in boiling water for 20 minutes, allow to cool, and then shred it prior to adding it to the lemon, chicken stock and potatoes. All depends on what kind of texture you want to create.

MINI WONTON SOUP IN GINGER GARLIC CHICKEN BROTH

Serves 2

Ingredients

3 cups chicken stock

⅓ cup soy sauce

½ cup chopped red onion

¼ cup prepared chopped garlic (or equal amount sliced fresh garlic)

2 tbsp minced ginger

2 tbsp sambal oleck or sambal badjak

2 tbsp chopped chives or green onions

Frozen mini wontons

4 tbsp olive oil

Preparation

Heat oil on medium heat in 2 ½ quart saucepan. Add onions and sauté about 2 minutes. Add garlic and ginger and stir. Add chicken stock, soy sauce and sambal, stir and bring to boil.

Add frozen mini wontons (6 per serving) and return to boil. Cook to instructions on package.

Serve in bowls and sprinkle with chives before serving.

MUSHROOM CHESTNUT WINTER SOUP

Serves 4

Ingredients

1½ lbs fresh chestnuts (Tip: if you want to save some serious time, you can substitute canned chestnuts and eliminate the entire first step of having to boil them)

1 large yellow onion (chopped)

6 tbsp butter

1 tbsp minced garlic

1 cup whole milk

½ tsp white wine vinegar

5 oz fresh white mushrooms (thinly sliced)

½ cup very thinly sliced carrots

2 tbsp olive oil

1 tsp salt

1 tsp pepper

2 cups chicken broth

Preparation

Boil the chestnuts for 20-25 minutes, drain and set aside in a bowl. (Skip this step if your chestnuts are canned.)

In a large frying pan, sauté the garlic and onion in butter over medium until lightly browned.

Add the chestnuts and sauté for 2-3 minutes.

Add the white wine vinegar and chicken broth. Add to this the milk and simmer, covered, for 10 minutes. Sprinkle in the salt and pepper and adjust to taste. Stir until creamy.

In a separate saucepan, sauté the sliced mushrooms and carrots in the olive oil for 2-3 minutes. Introduce the mushrooms and carrots to the soup and serve.

PINEAPPLE FRIED RICE

Serves 2

For this recipe, you can either make your white rice from the get-go or use any leftover rice you have from the last time you ordered Chinese takeout. The important thing to remember for this dish is

that the leftover rice has to be cold when you start cooking. I also use canned pineapple chunks instead of having to deal with the infrastructure of an entire fresh pineapple.

Ingredients

1 tbsp cooking oil

2 green onions (finely chopped)

1 tbsp minced garlic

1 cup of pineapple chunks (drained)

½ tsp grated ginger

1½ cups leftover white rice

2 tbsp soy sauce

½ cup fresh basil (chopped)

⅓ cup cashews

½ tbsp siracha

Preparation

In a large frying pan or wok, sauté the green onions, garlic and ginger in the cooking oil on medium heat for about a minute. Add the pineapple chunks, drop the heat to low and sauté for 4-5 minutes. The pineapple will turn light brownish.

Add the rice, soy sauce and sriracha and turn up the heat. Stir constantly for 3-5 minutes. The rice will take on a dry, crispy texture. Add the fresh basil and cashews for approximately 45 seconds and serve.

POTATO SALAD SICILIAN-STYLE

Serves 4-6

Ingredients

6 medium red potatoes

½ cup red onion (chopped)

1½ cups cherry tomatoes (halved)

1 jar (5 oz) pimento-stuffed olives, drained and cut in halves

3 tbsp minced garlic

2 tbsp balsamic

⅓ cup olive oil

½ tsp salt

½ tsp pepper

1 tsp dry oregano

4 large fresh basil leaves (chopped)

Preparation

Parboil the potatoes and cut into cubes.

In a large lidded bowl, mix all of the ingredients in with the potato cubes.

Put in the refrigerator and chill until ready to serve.

RED LENTIL SOUP

Serves 4

Ingredients

2 qts chicken stock

1 large yellow onion (diced)

1 lb red lentils

1 tbsp minced garlic

1 tbsp ground cumin

1 tsp cayenne pepper

½ cup fresh cilantro (chopped)

3 tbsp olive oil

2 tbsp fresh squeezed lemon juice

Preparation

In a large saucepan, heat the chicken stock and lentils to a boil. Reduce the heat to low and simmer covered for about 20 minutes.

In a skillet, heat the olive oil, garlic and onion. Sauté until the onion has softened.

Add the garlic and onion to the lentils and sprinkle with cayenne and cumin. Continue to stir for about 10 minutes more.

Pour this mixture into a blender and puree until creamy. Introduce the lemon juice and cilantro for the last phase and serve.

RUSTIC CLAM CHOWDER

If you live near the seashore and like to go clamming, good on you! You'll have access to fresh clams for this recipe. If not, there's absolutely nothing wrong with buying canned clams and clam juice.

Serves 4-6

Ingredients

6 strips of bacon, cut into 1-inch pieces

1 large yellow onion, diced

3 tbsp minced garlic

½ cup flour

3 cans of canned clams, finely chopped

4 cups clam juice

2 cups heavy whipping cream

2 lbs small red potatoes, peeled and cubed

2 tbsp fresh parsley or chives, chopped

Preparation

In a large stew pot, brown the bacon for about 10 minutes. Remove with a slotted spoon and place on paper towels to drain.

Sauté the garlic and onions on medium for 10 minutes. Introduce the flour and stir.

Pour in the clam juice and 2 cups of warm water. Add the potatoes. Simmer, covered, for approximately 20 minutes or until your potatoes have softened.

Introduce the clams, heavy cream, bacon and parsley or chives and heat for 3-4 minutes.

Serve with sourdough bread.

SPICY PEA SOUP

Serves 2

Ingredients

2 tbsp butter

2 tbsp chopped onion

2 cups frozen peas (drained)

½ tsp sugar

2 cups chicken stock

1 cup milk

½ tsp Herbs de Provence

1 tbsp ground jalapeno chiles (powder)

Pinch of black pepper

Flour (optional)

Directions

Melt butter in a large saucepan, add onion and sauté until transparent.

Add peas, sugar and chicken stock.

Cover and cook until the peas are tender.

Transfer to a food processor and puree.

Return the pureed peas to the saucepan.

Add a pinch of black pepper, the Herbs de Provence, the ground jalapeno chiles and the milk.

Mix thoroughly over medium heat.

Note: If you feel the soup is too thin, stir in flour 1 tsp at a time.

THE MINESTRONE

Christina and I have a funny story about minestrone. A few years before we met, a psychic friend of hers set her up on a date with an artist who painted his clients' auras. (Yes. Really. You cannot make these things up.) Although I do question why a legit psychic wouldn't have known this match-up was a disaster, my future wife always looks at such opportunities as free material for her novels and plays. He took her to an Italian restaurant and asked if she'd mind if he ordered for her. Sensitive to the fact that aura-painting probably doesn't pay very well, she agreed. He proceeded to order a small bowl of minestrone for her...and a three-course meal for himself. Suffice it to say, it was their one and only date. But, henceforth, every time we have gone to an Italian eatery, I always tease whether she'd like a bowl of minestrone. I love to hear her laugh.

Serves 4

Ingredients

2 cans of chicken broth

2 cans of tomato sauce

1 can of chickpeas (drained)

1 can of diced tomatoes

1 can of kidney beans (drained)

1 medium yellow onion, diced

2 stalks of celery, finely sliced

2 medium carrots, finely sliced

2 cups chopped cabbage (Note: save the time chopping and just buy it in a bag)

1 tbsp olive oil

2 tbsp butter

2 tbsp minced garlic

2 tsp dried parsley

1 tbsp dried basil

2 tsp dried oregano

2 tsp Italian herbs

1 cup elbow or shell macaroni (uncooked)

3 tsp grated Parmesan

Preparation

In a large saucepan, melt the butter and olive oil. Sauté the onion, carrots, celery and garlic for 3-4 minutes.

Introduce the chicken broth, tomato sauce, both cans of beans, the diced tomatoes, cabbage and spices. Cover and simmer for 15-20 minutes.

Add the uncooked pasta and cook for 7-8 minutes more, uncovered.

Pour into soup bowls and sprinkle with Parmesan to finish.

SEAFOOD

Seafood presents diverse opportunities to savor flavors from all over the world. As is the case with any other meal you are presenting for guests, be aware of any potential allergy someone in your party may have. Once, my wife and I were at a banquet in Northern California. The mashed potatoes served with the main course had a taste I could not identify. I asked the server what was in them and he replied, "lobster." I quickly looked around for a menu card—there was none—and said to my wife, "Well, that's a bit odd, isn't it?" As someone well versed in risk management issues, the evening could have ended on a deadly note if even one of the guests had a shellfish allergy. Note: Christina subsequently used this premise in one of the books in her UK cozy mystery series.

Fish can be served in any one of a number of ways—grilled, broiled, baked, fried, sautéed, or poached. Generally, fish falls into two categories: white fish and oily fish. White fish presents a wide range of textures and flavors, from mild and delicately flavored fish like snapper and sole, to firmer and more pronounced flavored fish like mahi-mahi and monkfish. The most common oily fish are salmon, swordfish and tuna, although anchovies also fall within this category. These fish are called "oily" because of a higher amount of beneficial oils throughout their bodies. In the case of swordfish, however, it is recommended to limit the amount one eats due to concerns about elevated levels of mercury in its meat. The same warning also is given to shark.

How to prepare your fish is in part determined by the fish you are preparing. As can be expected, grilling or broiling a delicate piece of snapper or tilapia will tend to make the fish firmer but drier if overcooked. A thicker white fish, such as sea bass or halibut, however, may stand up better to the high heat. The consensus for tuna is to sear the outside and preserve the inside rare or medium rare whether the tuna is grilled, broiled, or sautéed.

Fish stands up to a wide range of dry rubs, marinades, and sauces. What you use depends on the meal you are preparing and on the fish itself. A strong marinade, sauce, or salsa/chutney can overwhelm the fish and be at odds with the accompaniments to the meal. There are plenty of options, but a basic rule is to consider white wine, lemon, and herbs for cooking with more delicate fish, and robust dry rubs, peppers, and even red wines for cooking oily fish.

AHI WITH CAPERS

Serves 2

Ingredients

2 ahi steaks

⅓ cup dry white wine

2 tsp dried rosemary

2 tbsp minced garlic

2 tbsp olive oil

Italian breadcrumbs

2 tbsp lemon juice

1 tsp capers, drained

¼ tsp salt

¼ tsp pepper

Preparation

Salt and pepper the steaks.

Compose a marinade of white wine, rosemary, and garlic. Put the tuna steaks in a glass or plastic container or a plastic bag and marinate for an hour.

Take the steaks out of the marinade and pat dry. Sauté in olive oil (medium heat for 2-3 minutes each side), brushing the marinade onto the steaks while they cook. As the ahi finishes, heat two tablespoons of olive oil, add the capers and the lemon juice.

When the steaks are done, put on plate, sprinkle breadcrumbs over the ahi, and add the heated sauce.

This will be a tart sauce with the capers and lemon juice. Serve with your favorite pasta tossed in olive oil and garlic, or garlic mashed potatoes.

BAKED SEAFOOD TRIO

Serves 2

Ingredients

2 whitefish filets (i.e., halibut, orange roughy, dover sole)

6 prawns, sans shells and tails

6 large sea scallops

½ cup dry white wine

3 tbsp melted butter

2 tsp minced garlic

1 tbsp fresh squeezed lemon juice

½ tsp seafood seasoning (I like Red Lobster™ or Old Bay™)

¼ tsp salt

¼ tsp pepper

1 tbsp fresh parsley, chopped

Cooking spray

Preparation

Preheat oven to 425 degrees.

Spray the bottom and interior sides of a glass baking dish.

Lay the scallops, shrimp and white fish in the baking dish.

Blend the wine, melted butter and lemon juice in a small bowl and pour over the top of your seafood combo. Sprinkle with the seafood seasoning, garlic, salt and pepper.

Bake, uncovered, for approximately 10 minutes. Garnish with the fresh parsley.

BASIL AND BUTTER SALMON

Serves 4

Ingredients

4 boneless, skinless salmon filets

4 tbsp butter

2 tbsp garlic powder

2 tbsp dried basil

½ tsp salt

½ tsp cayenne

Lemon wedges for garnish

Preparation

Mix the basil, garlic, cayenne and salt in a bowl. Thoroughly coat both sides of the pieces of salmon.

In a large skillet, melt the butter on medium heat.

Add the salmon filets and cook for approximately 4 minutes on each side.

Plate and garish with the lemon.

Seriously, it was all that simple, wasn't it?

CHORIZO SALMON WITH TOMATOES AND BASIL

Serves 2

Ingredients

2 boneless, skinless salmon filets

10 oz tri-color cherry tomatoes, halved

1 oz chorizo (thinly sliced)

½ cup pitted black olives, halved

1 cup fresh basil leaves

3 tbsp olive oil

1 tbsp red wine vinegar

¼ tsp salt

¼ tsp pepper

Preparation

In a small bowl, mix the halved cherry tomatoes, olives, 1 tbsp olive oil, red wine vinegar, salt, pepper, and torn basil. Set aside.

In a skillet, heat the 2 tbsp of olive oil and cook the salmon filets, approximately 4 minutes each side. Remove to a plate and keep warm.

In the same skillet, introduce the chorizo and stir for 2-3 minutes. Add the tomatoes and olives for an additional minute.

On the plate, lay down the chorizo, tomatoes and olives and place the salmon filets on top.

COD FILETS IN MISO

You can substitute swordfish or mahi-mahi for the cod in this dish.

Serves 4

Ingredients

4 fresh cod filets (skin on)

3 tbsp mirin

3 tbsp sake

½ cup white miso (you can find this in the Asian section of your supermarket)

½ cup sugar

2 tbsp olive oil

1 tbsp butter

Preparation

In a small saucepan, bring the mirin and sake to a boil. Add the white miso and whisk for about a minute. Add the sugar and continue to stir for about 2 minutes.

Pour the mixture in a glass or ceramic dish for marinating and let it totally cool.

Add the cod filets to the marinade and completely coat both sides. Cover and leave in the fridge for 12-24 hours.

On the day of cooking, heat the oil and butter in a large frying pan. Introduce the filets, skin-side up, and cook for about 3 minutes.

Preheat oven to broil.

Flip the filets so they are now skin-side down, put the frying pan in the oven on a rack 8 inches from the top and broil for 5 minutes. This will result in a nice flaky fish with a sweet glaze on it.

FOIL-BAKED SALMON WITH TOMATOES

Clean-up really doesn't get any easier than this!

Serves 4

Ingredients

4 boneless, skinless salmon filets

3 Roma tomatoes, chopped

2 shallots, chopped

3 tbsp olive oil

2 tbsp fresh squeezed lemon juice

1 tsp thyme

1 tsp oregano

1 tsp garlic powder

¼ tsp salt

¼ tsp pepper

Preparation

Sprinkle both sides of the salmon filets with salt and pepper. Using a pastry brush, paint the top of each of the salmon pieces with 1 tbsp of the olive oil.

Mix the tomatoes, shallots, lemon juice and spices in a small bowl.

Preheat the onion to 400 degrees.

Cut 4 pieces of aluminum foil which will be large enough to encase each piece of salmon.

Place a salmon filet with the oiled side down in the middle of each piece of foil and generously spoon the tomato mixture over the top. Fold all four sides over the top of the salmon filet and crimp to seal. Do this with each piece.

Place the foil pockets on a baking sheet and bake for approximately 25 minutes.

The finished product can either be eaten directly out of the foil cribs or transferred to individual plates.

HONEY GARLIC SALMON FILETS

Serves 4

Ingredients

4 boneless, skinless salmon filets

4 tbsp minced garlic

4 tbsp honey

2 tbsp fresh lemon juice

3 tbsp butter

2 tsp soy sauce

¼ salt

¼ tsp pepper

¼ tsp smoky paprika

Preparation

Season both sides of the salmon filets with a mixture of salt, pepper and smoky paprika.

In a large pan on medium heat, melt the butter and sauté the minced garlic. Add the honey, soy sauce and lemon juice and stir constantly.

Add the salmon filets to the pan and cook on medium for approximately 4 minutes each side. To keep the filets moist while cooking, baste them with the juices they are cooking in.

Plate and serve atop a salad or alongside steamed rice.

LEMON AND LIME SHRIMP DRIZZLE

You can either do this dish as an appetizer or serve over white rice.

Serves 4

Ingredients

12 jumbo prawns, sans shells and tails

2 large lemons

2 large limes

3 tbsp minced garlic

3 tbsp chopped fresh parsley

3 tbsp olive oil

2 tbsp sherry

Preparation

Squeeze out the juice of the lemons and limes and set aside.

In a large skillet, heat the olive oil and sauté the garlic on medium.

Add the shrimp and stir briskly until they have turned pink. Remove from heat and add the juice and sherry.

Return to the stove and heat on low for an additional minute.

Plate the shrimp and sprinkle with the fresh parsley.

LEMON PEPPER MAHI-MAHI

A very simple dish which looks like you went to a lot more work than you actually did.

Serves 2

Ingredients

2 Mahi-Mahi filets(fresh or frozen)

⅓ cup lemon pepper marinade *(To save time, I use a commercial marinade such as Lawry's™, Kroger™ or World Harbors™)*

¼ cup panko breadcrumbs

Cooking spray

Fresh vegetables of your choice (slice zucchini and Italian squash are a colorful accompaniment)

Preparation

Place the Mahi-Mahi filets in a lidded dish and evenly pour the lemon pepper marinade over them. Refrigerate for two hours.

When you're ready to cook, preheat the oven to 325 degrees.

Sprinkle ¼ cup panko breadcrumbs on a flat dish. Coat both sides of each filet with the breadcrumbs.

Use cooking spray on a Pyrex or ceramic baking dish.

Place aluminum foil over the filets and bake for 20 minutes. Remove the foil and bake for an additional 5 minutes. By the by, those last 5 minutes are enough time to lightly sauté your favorite vegetables in butter and a smidge of seasoned salt.

MANGO TANGO SHRIMP

Serves 2

Ingredients

1 dozen large prawns sans shells and tails

6 tbsp minced garlic

2 tbsp commercial mango chutney

1 tbsp curry powder

1 quartered lime for garnish

1 tbsp olive oil

White rice

Preparation

In a large skillet, sauté the garlic in olive oil until aromatic. Sprinkle in the curry powder and stir.

Add the prawns and sauté for 4-5 minutes.

Add the mango chutney and continue to simmer on low for another 1-2 minutes.

Serve over white rice.

MUSTARD MAPLE SALMON

Serves 4

Ingredients

4 boneless, skinless salmon filets

4 tsp maple syrup

2 tbsp Dijon mustard

1 tbsp mayonnaise

2 tbsp fresh chopped dill

Preparation

In a small bowl, combine the maple syrup, mustard, mayonnaise and dill.

Line a large baking sheet with foil and preheat the oven to 400 degrees.

Place the salmon filets on the baking sheet and, using a pastry brush, generously coat the top of each salmon piece with the mixture you have just made.

Bake for 10-12 minutes.

Remove and plate.

PEPPERCORN PRAWNS

Serves 4

Ingredients

2 lbs prawns, sans shells and tails

2 cups whole milk

1 cup chicken stock

½ cup heavy whipping cream

4 tbsp butter

5 tbsp flour

3 tbsp dry sherry

1 tbsp drained peppercorns

½ tsp dry mustard

¼ tsp cayenne

Preparation

In a large skillet, heat the butter and flour on low heat for 2 minutes. Pour in the milk and the chicken stock, stirring constantly until it starts to thicken.

Introduce the mustard, cayenne, dry sherry and heavy whipping cream.

Lastly, add the prawns and the peppercorns and simmer until the prawns have turned pink.

I recommend serving over rice or pasta.

POACHED SALMON IN VERMOUTH

Hey, why not make yourself a martini while you're at it?

Serves 4

Ingredients

4 boneless, skinless salmon filets

1 cup dry vermouth

1 can quartered artichoke hearts, chopped

¼ cup water

3 tbsp fresh squeezed lemon juice

3 tbsp grated onion

1 tbsp butter

1 tbsp flour

¼ tsp salt

¼ tsp pepper

Preparation

In a large frying pan, gently poach the salmon filets in the vermouth, water and lemon juice. This should take about 7-8 minutes. Remove the filets from the liquid and keep warm on a separate, covered plate.

Pour the liquid from the poaching into a blender along with the chopped artichoke hearts, salt, pepper and onion. Blend until the mixture is smooth.

In the same frying pan you used previously, melt the butter and sprinkle in the flour. Pour the artichoke sauce into this and cook it down until the mixture is creamy.

Serve over the poached salmon.

PRAWN FLORENTINE

Serves 4

Ingredients

1 lb prawns, sans shells and tails

1 bag of baby spinach

½ large yellow onion, chopped

2 small zucchinis, thinly sliced (for visual variety, use yellow and green)

4 tbsp butter

1 tbsp olive oil

1 tbsp fresh squeezed lemon juice

2 tbsp minced garlic

2 tsp red pepper flakes

½ tsp salt

½ tsp pepper

Preparation

In a large skillet, heat 2 tbsp of the butter and the olive oil over medium. Sauté the zucchini, onion, garlic and salt for 4-5 minutes. Using a slotted spoon, remove to a separate plate.

Using the same skillet, add the rest of the butter and the prawns. Constantly stir until your prawns start to turn pink. Add the lemon juice, red pepper flakes, black pepper and the entire bag of baby spinach.

Sauté until the spinach starts to get wilty (this won't take very long!).

Add your zucchini and onion creation back into the skillet and heat for an additional 2 minutes.

Serve over pasta or rice.

ROSEMARY AND GARLIC PRAWNS

Serves 4

Ingredients

1 lb large prawns, sans shells and tails

3 tbsp olive oil

2 tbsp crushed garlic

4 tbsp butter

¾ cup dry vermouth

¼ tsp salt

¼ tsp pepper

2 tsp dry rosemary

Preparation

Combine the prawns, salt, pepper, olive oil, garlic and rosemary in a large lidded bowl. Shake thoroughly and marinate overnight in the fridge.

In a large skillet on medium-high, melt the butter and add the prawns plus marinade. Sauté for 2-3 minutes or until your prawns are pink. Remove with a slotted spoon to a separate plate.

With the pan off the stovetop, pour in the vermouth. Return to the heat and bring to a rapid boil.

Add the prawns back to the pan and stir brisky for 2 minutes prior to serving.

SALMON CROQUETTES

Paired with a mixed green salad, this recipe makes for a nice summer luncheon for 2-4 guests. You can also double all of the ingredients and turn it into party appetizers.

Ingredients

1 can (8 oz) salmon

1 egg

1 small onion (finely diced)

¾ cup Italian breadcrumbs

½ tsp salt

½ tsp pepper

A sprinkle of fresh parsley

Cooking oil

Preparation

The longest part of the prep is probably draining and flaking the salmon, then carefully combing through it to make sure there isn't any skin shrapnel or bones.

In a medium sized bowl, thoroughly combine the salmon, egg, onion, salt, pepper and breadcrumbs.

Using your hands, form the mixture into patties approximately two inches in diameter.

Pour enough cooking oil into a large skillet to cover the bottom. Heat to medium.

Fry the salmon patties for four minutes on each side to lightly brown them. Stove temperatures vary so be careful you don't get splattered.

Serve with a sprinkle of fresh parsley. For a nice dip, use tartar sauce, remoulade, or sour cream and dill.

SALMON FILETS IN VODKA SAUCE

Serves 4

Ingredients

4 boneless, skinless salmon filets

¾ cup vodka

1 large shallot, thinly sliced

1 tbsp minced garlic

4 tbsp olive oil

4 tbsp fresh lime juice

2 tbsp fresh parsley (chopped)

¼ tsp salt

¼ tsp pepper

Preparation

Mix together the lime juice, shallot and half the olive oil. Set aside while you prepare the salmon fillets.

Heat a large frying pan with the other half of the olive oil. Sprinkle salt and pepper on the salmon filets and sauté for approximately 4 minutes on each side. Transfer to a plate prior to serving.

In the same frying pan, add the garlic, lime juice mixture and vodka. Return to the stovetop and simmer until the liquid has reduced by half.

Plate the salmon and pour the vodka sauce over. Sprinkle parsley over the top for color.

SCALLOP AND SHRIMP GRATIN

Serves 2

Ingredients

10 oz peeled and deveined jumbo prawns

1 cup bay scallops

3 tbsp butter

2 tbsp flour

1 cup half & half

1 tbsp Dijon mustard

½ tsp. ground white pepper

2 tbsp white wine

1 tsp seafood seasoning*

½ cup grated Parmesan

1 cup grated Gruyere

Panko breadcrumbs

Finely chopped parsley (optional)

* There is a wide range of herb and spice blends that could be used for this recipe. My favorite is the French Seafood Seasoning from Vanns Spices™ (https://www.vannsspices.com/)

Preparation

Heat oven to 400 degrees

Sauté prawns and scallops in 1 tbsp of butter. Add wine and seasoning and cook until prawns are pink.

In a saucepan, melt remaining butter and heat until bubbling. Add flour and whisk until thickened. Slowly add half & half and continue to whisk until slightly thickened. Add white pepper and Dijon mustard and whisk until fully absorbed. Add Parmesan and stir.

Add the seafood to the gratin pans. Pour the sauce over the seafood. Sprinkle the grated Gruyere evenly over the seafood mixture and then cover with Panko breadcrumbs.

Bake for 15-20 minutes. Dish should be bubbling and breadcrumbs starting to brown.

Sprinkle with finely chopped parsley before serving.

SCALLOP AND VEGGIE PASTA

Serves 4

Ingredients

1 lb bay scallops

1 lb packaged fettucine or spaghetti

4 Roma tomatoes (chopped)

2 small zucchinis (chopped)

¼ cup olive oil

3 tbsp minced garlic

1 tbsp red pepper flakes

1 cup fresh basil (chopped)

3 tbsp grated Parmesan cheese

Preparation

Prepare the pasta per package instructions.

In a large frying pan, heat the oil and minced garlic until fragrant.

Add the zucchini and red pepper flakes. Sauté for 8 minutes on medium before adding the scallops, tomatoes and fresh basil. Simmer for an additional 5-7 minutes.

Ladle the scallop and veggie sauce over the pasta and top with Parmesan cheese.

SCALLOPS PROVENÇAL

Serves 4

Ingredients

1½ lbs of large sea scallops

2 cups canned plum tomatoes (drained and diced)

½ cup flour

2 tbsp olive oil

2 tbsp minced garlic

2 tbsp minced shallots

2 tbsp finely chopped parsley

⅔ cup dry vermouth

½ tsp brown sugar

½ cup grated Gruyere

½ cup garlic or Italian breadcrumbs

Salt and pepper

Preparation

Pat the scallops dry, cut into quarters and lightly season with salt and pepper.

Toss the scallops in flour, shaking off the excess. Heat the olive oil to medium high in a large frying pan.

Aggressively sauté the scallops for 1-2 minutes.

Add the tomatoes, vermouth, garlic, shallots, parsley and brown sugar. Continue to cook until the sauce thickens and all of the scallops are coated.

Mixed the grated cheese with the breadcrumbs.

Put the scallops in gratin pans and sprinkle cheese and breadcrumbs over the top. This can either be served immediately or placed under a broiler for 2 minutes to lightly brown and melt the cheese.

SCALLOPS WITH LIME AND SWEET CHILI BUTTER

Before I married Christina, I confess I was loathe to eating scallops. I can only put this down to probably tasting a badly cooked batch at some point in my life and aggressively avoiding them thereafter. My wife, however, was an expert when it came to bringing out the best in their flavor and texture and I have been a fan ever since.

Serves 2

Ingredients

12 large sea scallops (if bought frozen, the side muscles have already been removed for you)

3 tbsp softened unsalted butter

2 large limes

2 tbsp sweet chili sauce

1 tbsp green onion (minced)

Salt and pepper

Preparation

Pat the scallops dry and lightly season with salt and pepper. Set aside.

In a small bowl, lightly grate the lime until you have approximately 2 tsp of peel. Cut the limes into wedges and set aside.

Add the chili sauce, green onion and butter to the lime peel and thoroughly mix. Melt 1 tbsp of the butter mixture in a large frying pan over medium heat. Add the scallops and cook for 3 minutes. Carefully turn and cook for another 3 minutes.

Transfer to plates, spoon the remaining butter mixture over the scallops and squeeze the lime wedges over the top to finish.

SHERRY GARLIC SHRIMP

What's not to love about a dish that uses two entire sticks of butter?! In Ohio where I was born, I believe butter is one of the four basic food groups.

Serves 4

Ingredients

2 sticks butter

2 lbs Argentinian prawns, sans shells and tails

1 cup Italian breadcrumbs

2 tbsp minced garlic

1 shallot, finely minced

¾ cup sherry

2 tbsp fresh tarragon, finely chopped

¼ cup fresh parsley, finely chopped

1 tsp ground nutmeg

½ tsp salt

½ tsp pepper

Preparation

In a medium bowl, mix one of the sticks of butter with the sherry, breadcrumbs, garlic, shallot, parsley, salt, pepper and nutmeg.

Preheat your oven to 425.

In a large baking dish, cut the remaining stick of butter into ¼ inch squares and place them on the bottom of the baking dish. (Isn't this fun?)

Put the prawns on top of the butter squares (it's all right if they overlap).

Pour the breadcrumb mixture you have made over the top of the prawns.

Bake for 10-25 minutes on the middle rack of the oven.

For the last step, turn the broiler on for 2-3 minutes.

SHRIMP AND MUSHROOMS WITH SHERRY CREAM SAUCE

Once upon a time if you were making a seafood dish, you had to buy the seafood fresh and then use it *immediately*. Nowadays you can keep a supply of frozen shrimp, scallops, salmon, etc. and take it out whenever you are ready.

Serves 2

Ingredients

10 oz large shrimp (tail off, peeled, deveined)

1 tbsp olive oil

2 tbsp butter

1 tbsp garlic powder

¼ tsp turmeric

1 cup dry sherry

1 cup thinly sliced fresh white mushrooms

½ cup heavy whipping cream

Dry chili pepper flakes and parsley

1 cup steamed white rice

Preparation

Sauté the shrimp in olive oil, butter, garlic powder and turmeric for approximately 5 minutes.

Start preparing the cup of white steamed rice. (If you're lazy, there'd nothing wrong with buying Minute Rice™ microwaveable.)

Add the sherry, mushrooms and heavy whipping cream. Stir to mix thoroughly. Cover and simmer on low until the rice is done.

Ladle the shrimp and mushrooms over the rice. Be generous with the sauce, as it will turn the rice into a risotto-like quality. Sprinkle dry chili pepper flakes and parsley over the top for a splash of color.

SHRIMP AND SCALLOP CURRY

Serves 4

Ingredients

12 sea scallops, halved

12 prawns, sans shells and tails

1 cup fresh asparagus, cut into 1-inch pieces

1 medium yellow onion, thinly sliced

1 can coconut milk

1 tbsp brown sugar

1 tbsp garlic, minced

1 tbsp ginger, minced

3 tbsp red curry paste

3 tbsp fresh squeezed lime juice

2 tbsp vegetable oil

2 tbsp fresh cilantro, finely chopped

Preparation

In a large frying pan or wok, heat the oil to medium and sauté the onion, garlic and ginger for 3 minutes.

Introduce the coconut milk, brown sugar, lime juice and curry paste. Bring to a nice shimmer and continue to stir for about 5 minutes.

Add the shrimp, scallops and cilantro and stir for 4-5 minutes on medium. Add the asparagus last and stir for an additional minute.

SHRIMP FETTUCINE ALFREDO

Sure you can buy any number of jars of pre-mixed Alfredo sauce but why would you want to when your own version can be so much dreamier and creamier?

Serves 4

Ingredients

1 package fettucine noodles

1 lb medium shrimp (peeled, deveined and tails off)

½ cup butter

1-½ cups heavy whipping cream

1 cup grated Parmesan cheese

1 tbsp spoon minced garlic

½ tsp pepper

1 tsp nutmeg

1 tbsp fresh parsley for garnish

Preparation

Prepare the fettuccine per package instructions.

In a large frying pan, melt the butter over medium heat and slowly introduce the heavy whipping cream. Sprinkle in the nutmeg.

Reduce the heat to low and add the shrimp, garlic and pepper, stirring constantly for about 3 minutes.

Drain the pasta and introduce the shrimp, garlic, pepper and Parmesan.

Plate the pasta and garnish with parsley.

SHRIMP PESTO

Serves 2 (or 4 if used as an appetizer)

Ingredients

12 oz peeled, deveined and tail-less large shrimp

2 tbsp olive oil

2 tbsp butter

2 tbsp garlic powder

3 tbsp basil pesto

Angel hair pasta

Preparation

Sauté the shrimp in the oil, butter and garlic powder on medium for approximately 10 minutes.

Reduce the heat and stir in the basil pesto, mixing throughout.

Prepare the angel hair pasta per package instructions.

Note: Angel hair cooks incredibly fast after you add it to boiling water. If you let it cook for more than two minutes, it is going to be a gloppy mess.

Drain the pasta, put on plates and spoon the shrimp pesto over it.

SHRIMP SCAMPI IN CILANTRO LIME

Serves 4

Ingredients

2 lbs of peeled, deveined and tail-less prawns

5 tbsp chopped garlic

¼ cup butter

¼ cup olive oil

1 tbsp crushed red pepper

¾ cup fresh cilantro (chopped)

4 tbsp Tequila (feel free to make yourself a Margarita while you're cooking!)

4 tbsp fresh lime juice

½ tsp salt

½ tsp pepper

Preparation

In a large frying pan, heat the butter, olive oil, half of the cilantro, garlic and red pepper. Stir constantly for about 2 minutes and remove from heat.

Add the Tequila a tablespoon at a time. Return to the stovetop and heat on medium until the liquid has evaporated. (If your Margarita has also evaporated, make yourself another!)

Add the shrimp, salt and pepper and the rest of the cilantro and sauté for about 5 minutes or until the shrimp have turned opaque. Stir in the fresh lime juice. Serve.

This dish can be enjoyed over pasta or rice or with sourdough baguettes.

SPAGHETTI WITH TUNA

Christina has always excelled at dishes which can be made in advance and then "voila!" put together for company on a moment's notice. Even better, this particular dish is easy to clean up because it only involves washing the pot in which the pasta was boiled.

Serves 4

Ingredients

1 large can of chunk white tuna (drained)*

2 tbsp anchovy paste

1 cup virgin olive oil

1 cup of chopped parsley

½ cup of crème fraiche

1 lb dry spaghetti

3 tbsp butter

½ cup sliced black olives

Salt and pepper to taste

Preparation

Put the tuna, anchovy paste, parsley and oil into a food processor and blend until the mixture is smooth. Give it a taste. If you think it needs a little more zip, add some salt and pepper or another squirt of anchovy paste.

Add the crème fraiche and blend some more. (This part of the recipe can be made in advance and stored in the refrigerator until you're ready to cook the pasta.)

In a large pot, prepare the spaghetti per package instructions. After draining the cooked pasta, return it to the pot and add the butter. After the butter has melted, add the sauce you've made and mix it all together.

Once you have put the pasta onto serving plates, garnish with black olives.

*Make sure the tuna is the kind packed in water, not oil, given the amount of oil added to the recipe.

SWEET AND SOUR SHRIMP

Serves 4

Ingredients

1 lb large shrimp, sans shells and tails

½ cup ketchup

½ cup Chinese plum sauce

1 tbsp finely chopped garlic

3 tbsp soy sauce

1 tsp fresh ginger, finely chopped

½ tsp crushed red pepper flakes

¼ tsp salt

¼ tsp pepper

2 thinly sliced scallions

3 tbsp rice wine vinegar

1 tbsp peanut oil

Preparation

In a small bowl, thoroughly mix the ketchup, Chinese plum sauce, soy sauce and red pepper flakes.

Sprinkle the shrimp with salt and pepper.

Using a large skillet or Asian wok, heat the peanut oil over medium. Sauté the shrimp in this for about three minutes. Using a slotted spoon, remove the shrimp from the skillet or wok.

Now sauté the garlic, ginger and sliced scallions over medium. Add the rice wine vinegar.

Next, add the mixture you made in the first step and bring this to a nice simmer.

Re-introduce the shrimp and sauté on low for 2-3 more minutes. Either serve as an appetizer or over steamed white rice.

SZECHUAN PRAWNS

This is a version of Kung Pao prawns that puts more emphasis on the prawns than on the sauce. This is intended to be prepared using a grill pan and then lightly coating the prawns in a prepared spicy sauce. Our favorites are House of Tsang Szechuan Spicy Stir-Fry Sauce™ or San-J Szechuan Hot & Spicy Marinade & Stir-Fry Gluten Free Sauce.™ While traditional Kung Pao dishes use peanuts, I use whole cashews (Planters™ salted), but peanuts are fine in this dish. As is always the case with nuts, make certain any guests are screened for allergies.

Serves 2

Ingredients

1 lb. Jumbo Prawns peeled and deveined (prefer tails off)

4 tbsp sesame chili oil

Szechuan pepper, ground

1 cup commercial Szechuan sauce (see notes above)

I cup salted cashews

1 cup steamed rice

Green onion tops, sliced

Preparation

Rub prawns in chili oil and coat liberally with ground Szechuan pepper. Thread onto moistened bamboo skewers

Heat grill pan to medium. When hot, place skewers on pan. Grill until done, but not overcooked. A grill press will speed up the cooking and keep the prawns at their desired consistency. Noting that this is at medium heat, I usually do three minutes per side and then quickly turn if more time is needs.

In a large pan, heat the Szechuan sauce. Slide the prawns off the skewers and coat with the sauce. Add the cashews (peanuts) and serve immediately over steamed rice. Top with sliced green onions.

If you or your guests like this spicier, serve some sambal oleck or chili-garlic sauce on the side and add while eating.

TUNA WITH FRESH PLUMS

Serves 4

Ingredients

4 tuna steaks

4 plums, quartered

¾ cup dry white wine

½ cup olive oil

1 tbsp olive oil

1 tbsp fresh lemon juice

1 tbsp maple syrup

1 tbsp finely chopped thyme

3 tbsp shaved Parmesan

2 tbsp Dijon mustard

Preparation

In a small bowl, whisk the ½ cup of olive oil with the wine, Dijon and thyme. Pour into a shallow baking dish.

Add the tuna steaks, turn on both sides to saturate and refrigerate for 15-20 minutes.

In a large frying pan, heat the 1 tbsp of olive oil to medium/high. Add the tuna steaks and cook 3 minutes per side. Remove to a separate plate.

In the same frying pan, add the quartered plums and sauté for 3-4 minutes. Introduce the fresh lemon juice and maple syrup, stirring for an additional minute.

Plate the tuna, spoon the plum sauce over them and sprinkle with the shaved Parmesan to finish.

WHITEFISH IN DREAMY CREAM SAUCE

I recommend haddock, pollock or filet of sole for this dish, all of which can be purchased fresh or frozen at your neighborhood grocery store.

Serves 4

Ingredients

4 whitefish filets

2 small medium yellow onions, sliced thin

3 tbsp butter

¼ cup olive oil

½ cup heavy whipping cream

¾ cup green onion, finely chopped

¼ cup parsley, finely chopped

½ tsp sweet paprika

½ cup carrot, sliced very thin

Preparation

Melt the butter and the olive oil in a large saucepan. Sauté the onion over medium for 6-7 minutes.

Introduce the whitefish filets. Cover the saucepan and simmer for 10 minutes.

Meanwhile, whisk together the heavy cream, green onion, parsley and paprika. Your finished sauce should be smooth and creamy.

Spoon this sauce along with the thin carrot slices over the fish filets, lower the heat and continue to simmer for another 5 minutes.

Plate and serve immediately.

FOWL PLAY

"Tastes like chicken." This well-worn phrase is generally not considered a compliment, although it can be descriptive for more exotic fare like rattlesnake. Poultry in general and chicken in particular is used in cuisines throughout the world. It lends itself to every possible type of preparation and presentation. Given the variety of ways chicken, duck and turkey are packaged, for example, a meal for two can be as easy to create as one for a family gathering.

I do have to say I'm not fond of cookbook recipes which call for a whole chicken. If you have the time, tools and inclination to disassemble the entire bird on your kitchen counter and parse out the parts you need for a particular meal, I'm very happy for you. My own preference is to buy the breasts, cutlets, thighs, wings and drumsticks either fresh or frozen and have that portion of the job already neatly done.

As for that Thanksgiving or Christmas turkey, Christina and I are usually guests at someone else's house (wherein I am the designated Wine Guy) or it's just the two of us at home. For the latter, a three-pound boneless turkey breast is all we really need for a tasty dinner...and plenty of leftovers for sandwiches!

AUTUMN CHICKEN

This seemed as good a name as any since it conjures thoughts of falling leaves, crisp nights and a cozy fire in the fireplace.

Serves 4

Ingredients

4 thinly sliced boneless, skinless chicken breasts

½ cup dry white wine

½ cup chicken broth

½ cup heavy whipping cream

4 tbsp minced garlic

2 small shallots, finely chopped

½ cup sundried tomatoes, finely chopped

1 tsp red pepper flakes

1 tbsp tomato paste

¼ tsp salt

¼ tsp pepper

1 tsp dried oregano

1 tsp dried thyme

1 tsp balsamic vinegar

2 tbsp olive oil

2 tbsp butter

1 cup grated Parmesan

Preparation

In a large frying pan on medium, heat the oil and 1 tbsp butter. Season the chicken breasts with the salt and pepper. Brown the chicken on both sides for about 3 minutes. Transfer to a plate and keep warm.

In the same frying pan on low, add the chopped shallots, oregano, thyme and red pepper flakes. Add the 3-minute mark, introduce the garlic, sun-dried tomatoes and tomato paste.

BLACK AND WHITE SESAME CHICKEN

So named for the finishing sprinkle of black poppy seeds and white sesame seeds.

Serves 4

Ingredients

4 boneless, skinless chicken breasts cut into bite-sized pieces

4 oz fresh white mushrooms, sliced

1 green or red bell pepper, seeded and sliced into strips

2 tbsp rice wine

2 tbsp soy sauce

1 tbsp minced garlic

1 tbsp fresh ginger, grated

1 tbsp fresh lemon juice

2 tsp cornstarch

2 tbsp vegetable oil

1 tbsp sesame oil

4 green onions cut into strips

1 tbsp sesame seeds

1 tbsp black poppy seeds

Steamed rice

Preparation

In a large covered bowl, thoroughly mix the rice wine, cornstarch, lemon juice, soy sauce, garlic and grated ginger. Add the chicken pieces. Put the lid on the bowl and give it a few shakes. Refrigerate for 4 hours.

On the day of cooking, heat the sesame oil and vegetable oil in a large frying pan or wok on low.

Using a slotted spoon, plop the chicken into the wok but reserve the marinade. Stir fry until the chicken pieces have all nicely browned. Remove chicken to a separate plate for the time being.

In the same wok and in the same oil, sauté the mushrooms, green onions and bell pepper strips for 2-3 minutes.

Add the chicken back in along with the reserved marinade. Plate the meal over steamed white rice and sprinkle an even distribution of black poppy seeds and white sesame seeds.

BLACKENED CHICKEN

Serves 2

Ingredients

2 boneless, skinless chicken breasts

½ tsp paprika

½ tsp cayenne pepper

¼ tsp dried thyme

¼ tsp ground cumin

¼ tsp onion powder

2 tbsp cooking oil

Respective dashes of salt and pepper

Cooking spray

Preparation

Preheat the oven to 375 degrees.

Combine all of the spices in a small mixing bowl.

Heat the oil to medium in a large frying pan.

Thoroughly coat both chicken breasts with the spice mixture.

Heat the chicken breasts in the frying pan, two minutes on each side.

Spray a ceramic baking dish with cooking spray.

Place the chicken breasts in the baking dish and bake for 15 minutes. (Add an additional 5 if the chicken breasts are particularly thick.)

BLANCO CHICKEN CHILI

Serves 4

Ingredients

3 boneless, skinless chicken breasts, quartered

1 large yellow onion, chopped

2 cans of cannellini beans, drained

5 cups of chicken broth

1 jalapeno, seeded and finely chopped

3 tbsp minced garlic

2 small cans of green chiles

1 cup frozen corn

½ cup sour cream

1 tsp dried oregano

1 tsp ground cumin

2 tbsp olive oil

¼ tsp salt

¼ tsp pepper

Preparation

In a large cooking pot, heat the olive oil to medium and sauté the onion, jalapeno, garlic and cumin for 6-8 minutes.

Add the chicken, green chiles, chicken broth, and salt and pepper. Simmer uncovered for 12-15 minutes.

Using a slotted spoon, remove the chicken only to a separate plate and shred with a pair of large forks.

In the same pot, add the beans and simmer for 10 minutes. Reintroduce the shredded chicken along with the corn and heat for two more minutes.

Dollop in the sour cream and continue stirring for another minute to thoroughly mix.

Serve in bowls with tortilla chips alongside.

BUTTER CHICKEN ALA FLORENTINE

Serves 2

Ingredients

2 boneless, skinless chicken breasts

¼ cup flour

1 egg

¼ cup fresh squeezed lemon juice

3 tbsp olive oil

¾ cup butter

¼ cup dry white wine

¼ tsp salt

¼ tsp pepper

Preparation

If the chicken breasts are on the thick side, gently pound them to ¾ inch prior to cooking.

Mix the flour, salt and pepper and spread out on a plate.

Break the egg into a small bowl and whisk. Using a pastry brush, coat the chicken breasts with egg and then dredge in the flour.

In a large frying pan, melt ½ cup of butter over medium heat until it starts to turn bubbly brown.

Put the chicken in the pan and cook both sides for 5-6 minutes each. When you turn the chicken to do the other side, add the rest of the butter and the white wine.

Drizzle the lemon juice over the top of the chicken and plate immediately.

Serve over pasta or wilted spinach.

CAJUN BOURBON CHICKEN

The origin of this Southern dish is supposedly the fusion of Chinese food and a popular New Orleans chicken recipe wherein the primary ingredient was bourbon. It might also be assumed that a lot of the latter was consumed during the cooking process which led to the meat becoming more tender and the chef becoming more—um—relaxed.

Serves 4

Ingredients

6 chicken thighs (boneless and skinless) cut into bite-sized pieces

3 tbsp cornstarch

2 tbsp olive oil

¼ cup bourbon

¼ cup brown sugar

¼ cup apple juice

¼ cup chicken broth

2 tbsp honey

2 tbsp ketchup

2 tbsp soy sauce

2 tsp apple cider vinegar

½ tsp ginger

½ tsp onion powder

¼ tsp salt

¼ tsp pepper

3 thinly sliced scallions

Steamed white rice (to save time I actually buy Minute Rice™ cups which can be microwaved)

Preparation

Mix the chicken, salt, pepper and half the cornstarch in a bowl. Heat the olive oil in a large pan and sauté the chicken until nicely browned. Remove to a plate. In a separate bowl, thoroughly whisk together the bourbon, chicken broth, brown sugar, apple juice, apple cider vinegar, honey, ketchup, soy sauce, ginger and onion power. Pour this sauce mixture into the same pan where you cooked the chicken and bring it to a boil. Reduce the heat to medium, add the chicken and continuously stir.

In a small bowl, add about 1-½ tsp of warm water to the remaining cornstarch and introduce it to the sauce to help thicken it (about a minute). Spoon the chicken over steamed white rice and sprinkle with chopped scallions.

CHICKEN AND ASPARAGUS PASTA

Seriously, any type of pasta will work with this dish but I have a fondness for penne and conchiglia (shells) myself because of the nice grip they make on the sauce.

Serves 4

Ingredients

1 lb boneless, skinless chicken thighs

1 package dry pasta

1 lb trimmed fresh asparagus cut into 1½ inch pieces

2 tbsp olive oil

3 tbsp butter

3 tbsp minced garlic

1 tsp red chili flakes

1½ cups dry white wine

½ fresh squeezed lemon juice

½ cup grated Parmesan

Preparation

Cut the chicken thighs into bite-size pieces. (Tip: It is easier to orchestrate this when they are semi-frozen).

Start boiling the water in which you will cook the pasta. Prepare pasta per package instructions.

In a large frying pan, heat the olive oil and sauté the chicken until it is lightly browned. Add the asparagus and continue to sauté on low.

In a separate saucepan, melt the butter and add to it the garlic, wine, chili flakes and lemon juice. Bring it to a boil, then reduce the heat.

When the pasta is ready and you are draining it, remove approximately 1 cup of the pasta water and add it to the sauce. Cook for about a minute, then pour the sauce over the drained pasta. Introduce the chicken and asparagus and thoroughly mix prior to plating.

Sprinkle grated Parmesan over the top and serve.

CHICKEN CORDON BLEU

This dish is much easier to make than one would think. Even better, you can assemble everything in advance—and also clean-up—thus, giving you more time to spend with your guests. Earlier versions of this recipe found in cookbooks involved deep-frying (which also tended to be potentially more messy). In a health-conscious world, the new way to do it is to bake it in the oven.

Serves 4

Ingredients

4 large boneless, skinless chicken breasts

4 slices Swiss cheese

4 slices of thinly sliced ham

1 egg

¼ tsp salt

¼ tsp pepper

1 cup Italian breadcrumbs

Cooking spray

Preparation

Pound the chicken breasts to ¼ inch thickness. If you have an especially nice butcher, this can be done for you.

Sprinkle the chicken breasts with salt and pepper.

Place one slice of cheese and one slice of ham in the center of each chicken breast.

Roll these up and either tuck in the ends or secure with toothpicks.

Whisk the egg and, using a pastry brush, coat each rolled chicken breast.

Generously roll in breadcrumbs.

Place covered in refrigerator until you're ready to cook.

Preheat oven to 350 degrees. Bake uncovered for 35-40 minutes.

Remove the toothpicks and serve.

CHICKEN KIEV

Serves 4

Ingredients

4 boneless, skinless chicken breasts pounded to ¼ inch thickness

4 eggs

1 cup flour

¾ cup softened salted butter

1 tbsp chopped fresh chives

1tbsp chopped fresh parsley

½ tsp dried thyme

1 tbsp minced garlic

1 tbsp Dijon mustard

1 cup Italian breadcrumbs

Cooking spray

Preparation

Mix together the softened butter and all of the herbs and garlic. Shape into a butter-shaped long cube, encase in plastic wrap and freeze until firm (approximately half an hour).

Whisk together the eggs and Dijon.

Lay the chicken breasts on a large cutting board. With the herbed butter cube you previously created, cut four equal slices and place one in the center of each chicken breast. Roll each chicken breast up around its precious butter cargo, tuck in the ends and secure with toothpicks.

Spread the flour on a plate and dredge each chicken roll in it.

"Paint" each of the chicken breasts with the egg and Dijon mixture. Lastly, roll each one in the Italian breadcrumbs to completely coat.

Preheat oven to 425 degrees.

Spray the bottom of the baking dish you plan to use and place the chicken breasts on it.

Bake for 30-35 minutes.

CHICKEN PICCATA

Serves 4

Ingredients

4 boneless, skinless chicken cutlets (Tip: you can also use chicken breasts but you'll need to slice or pound them to ¼ inch thinness for best cooking results.)

½ cup all-purpose flour

3 tbsp olive oil

3 tbsp fresh lemon juice

½ cup dry white wine

2 tbsp minced garlic

1 tbsp capers

1 pinch each of salt and pepper

Preparation

Add the pinches of salt and pepper to the flour and mix.

Dredge the chicken cutlets in the flour and shake off the excess.

Heat the olive oil to medium in a large skillet.

Lightly brown the chicken cutlets (1-2 minutes per side). Remove to a separate plate.

In the same pan, add the lemon juice, capers, minced garlic and white wine. Bring to a boil over medium for about 10 minutes.

Plunk the chickened cutlets into the sauce and simmer, covered, for 10 more minutes.

Plate the chicken and pour the remaining sauce over it. This disk works well with either pasta or mashed potatoes.

CHICKEN THIGHS WITH LEMONS AND CARROTS

Serves 4

Ingredients

8 chicken thighs (skin-on)

1 lb fresh carrots cut into 1-inch pieces (baby carrots sliced lengthwise are also charming for this dish)

2 cups chicken broth

2 tbsp butter

3 tbsp flour

1 large lemon, thinly sliced

5 sprigs of fresh thyme

2 tsp paprika

¼ tsp salt

¼ tsp pepper

Preparation

Rub the chicken thighs with the paprika, salt and pepper.

Heat the butter in a large frying pan. Place the chicken with the skin-side facing down and brown for about 6 minutes. (Do not flip the chicken over!) Remove the thighs to a separate plate.

In the same pan, heat the carrots until they have browned (about 6-7 minutes). Sprinkle the flour into the skillet and continue to stir. Now add the chicken broth and the sprigs of thyme and bring to a boil.

Reintroduce the chicken to the skillet, this time with the skin facing up, and lay them on top of the carrots. Put a lid on the skillet and allow to continue cooking on low for 20 minutes. At the end of that time, remove the thyme sprigs and discard. Add the lemon slices on top of the chicken and heat for an additional 2 minutes.

This dish works well with mashed potatoes as a side or atop your favorite pasta.

CHICKEN WITH MUSHROOM-COGNAC SAUCE

Serves 4

Ingredients

4 thick chicken breasts cut into large chunks

1 cup heavy whipping cream

4 tbsp butter

½ lb white mushrooms, sliced thin

½ lb shitake mushrooms, sliced thin

1 cup dry white wine

1 cup chicken stock

2 tsp Herbs de Provence

3 tbsp Cognac

1 tbsp tarragon (finely chopped)

1 tsp salt

1 tsp pepper

Preparation

In a large skillet sauté the chicken in the butter along with the Herbs de Provence, salt and pepper. The chicken should be a nice, light brown. Using a slotted spoon, remove the chicken to a separate plate.

In the same skillet, introduce the mushrooms and sauté on low heat for 10-15 minutes. Add the wine and chicken stock and simmer for 5 minutes. Now add the cream and Cognac. (Note: Briefly remove the skillet from the heat *before* you pour in the Cognac, just to be on the safe side.) Continue to stir until the sauce thickens. Sprinkle in the tarragon.

Return the chicken to the skillet and stir for 15 minutes, allowing the pieces to soak up all of this lovely mushroom sauce.

Serve and sit back to enjoy the compliments.

CHICKEN WITH MUSTARD DILL SAUCE

Serves 4

Ingredients

4 boneless, skinless chicken breasts

¼ cup flour

3 tbsp oil

½ tsp salt

½ tsp black pepper

½ cup finely chopped shallots

1 cup dry white wine

1 cup chicken broth

4 tsp coarse-grain mustard

¼ fresh fill (finely chopped)

Preparation

Mix together the flour, salt and pepper in a shallow bowl. Pat the chicken breasts dry and dredge each in the flour mixture. Set aside.

Heat the oil in a large frying pan to medium heat. Brown the chicken breasts approximately 6 minutes each side. Remove to a separate plate.

In the same pan, sauté the shallots. Add the wine, chicken broth and mustard. Bring the heat to a simmer and return the chicken breasts to the frying pan. Cover over moderate heat for about 25 minutes.

Remove the chicken breasts to plates and bring the remaining liquid to a boil until it has nicely thickened. Stir in the fresh dill and ladle over the chicken prior to serving.

CHICKEN WITH SAGE AND MUSHROOMS

Serves 4

Ingredients

4 large skinned and boneless chicken breasts

1 cup chopped shallots

2 tbsp garlic, minced

1 lb fresh mushrooms, chopped

⅓ cup sherry

3 tbsp flour

½ cup butter

1 package of wild rice

2 (14 oz) cans of unsalted chicken broth

½ cup Parmesan, grated

½ tsp salt

½ tsp pepper

2 tbsp fresh sage (chopped)

2 tbsp fresh parsley (chopped)

Cooking spray

Preparation

Melt ¼ cup of the butter in a large skillet on medium. Sauté the chicken until lightly browned. Using a slotted spoon, remove the chicken to a separate plate.

In the same skillet, sauté the shallots and garlic. Introduce the mushrooms and continue stirring for about 5 minutes. Add the sherry and stir for an additional minute.

In a separate saucepan, melt the remaining butter and whisk in the flour. Add the broth and bring to a boil. After 1-2 minutes, this mixture will start to thicken. Remove the saucepan from the heat and add the package of rice. No add the Parmesan, salt, pepper, sage and parsley, as well as the shallot and garlic sauce you previously made.

Preheat oven to 375 degrees. Lightly spray a baking dish and pour everything into it. Lastly, top with the chicken breasts. Bake for 35-40 minutes.

Note: Something fun to serve as a side with this dish is some StoveTop™ stuffing embellished with some additional sage seasoning.

CHRISTINA'S VIENNESE PAPRIKA CHICKEN

Serves 2

Ingredients

2 small boneless/skinless chicken breasts

1 small chopped yellow onion

¼ cup flour

1½ cup beef stock

1 cup sour cream

2 tbsp olive oil

2 tbsp sweet paprika powder

1 tbsp fresh dried parsley

Wide egg noodles

Preparation

Cut the chicken into bite-sized pieces.

Brown the chicken and onion in olive oil.

Add the paprika.

Add half of the beef stock.

Dust with flour and slowly stir in the sour cream.

Add the rest of the beef stock, reduce heat and let the mixture simmer, stirring occasionally.

Note: If you would like the sauce thicker, add more flour; if you would like it thinner, add more beef stock.

Prepare the egg noodles per package instructions.

To serve, ladle the paprika chicken over the noodles and sprinkle with parsley.

COQ AU VIN

Serves 4

Ingredients

4 chicken thighs (skin on)

8 slices of bacon, cut into 1-inch pieces

½ cup diced yellow onion

1 dozen button mushrooms, quartered

2 cups red wine

1 cup chicken broth

2 tsp butter

2 tsp flour

2 tsp fresh thyme, chopped

2 shallots, thinly sliced

¼ tsp salt

¼ tsp pepper

Preparation

Season the chicken thighs with the salt and pepper.

In a large, oven-proof skillet, sauté the bacon pieces over medium for 10-15 minutes. Remove with a slotted spoon to dry on paper towels.

Place the chicken thighs with the skin down in the skillet with the bacon drippings. Cook for 2-3 minutes on each side until nicely browned. Remove from the skillet to a separate plate.

Lower the heat and sauté the button mushrooms, diced onion and shallots for about 8 minutes.

Preheat the oven to 375 degrees.

Sprinkle in the flour. Add the red wine and bring to a boil.

Return the bacon pieces to the skillet along with the chopped thyme. Reduce the heat and allow to simmer until the wine has reduced (approximately 5 minutes).

Introduce the chicken stock. Add the chicken thighs. After two minutes of simmering on the stovetop, transfer the skillet to the middle rack of your oven and cook for half an hour. Periodically spoon the juices over the chicken thighs to keep them moist. Reduce the heat to 300 degrees and cook for an additional 20 minutes.

DUCK WITH APRICOTS

Serves 4

This is a wonderfully aromatic dish and not that difficult to fix. Once we moved to Dobbs Mill, however, our duck days were over. Christina had befriended two endearing ducks on our lake and named them Terrence and Sebastian. Heaven forbid she should ever go out to feed them and they might catch a whiff of a possible relative on her breath. Horrors!

Ingredients

4 duck breasts cut into serving pieces

½ small yellow onion (chopped)

3 tbsp garlic (minced)

1 tbsp sweet paprika

1 plum tomato or 6 cherry tomatoes (diced)

2-½ cups chicken broth

3 tbsp olive oil

½ cup chorizo (thinly sliced)

¼ cup dry apricots

¼ cup sliced olives (I recommend Kalamata)

1 cup arborio rice

Preparation

Heat the oil and garlic in a large frying pan and cook over low heat for approximately 5 minutes.

Add the tomato and paprika and stir for about 5 minutes until the tomato has nicely softened.

Add the arborio rice and half the chicken stock. Stir and simmer on low for about 8 minutes.

Introduce the duck, chorizo, dried apricots and olives. Pour in the other half of the chicken broth and bring to a boil.

Preheat the oven to 375. Place the uncovered skillet in the oven and allow it to bake for around 16 minutes by which time the arborio rice will have soaked up all of the liquid in the pan.

FLORENTINE CHICKEN MARSALA

Serves 4

Ingredients

4 chicken breasts (boneless and skinless)

1 cup sun-dried tomatoes

1 cup fresh spinach (chopped)

1 cup Marsala wine

1 cup butter

¼ cup flour

3 cups portabella mushrooms (thinly sliced)

2 tbsp olive oil

1 tbsp dry oregano

¼ tsp each salt and pepper

Preparation

Pound the chicken breasts to ¼ inch thick (Note: If you eschew pounding, you can always buy thinly sliced chicken breasts at the store.)

Mix the flour, oregano, salt and pepper and dust the chicken breasts.

Fry the chicken in olive oil on medium (approximately three minutes each side). Set aside.

In the same frying pan, heat the butter, mushrooms, sun-dried tomatoes and wine. Stir about for 10 minutes, then add the spinach. Cook for an additional 2-3 minutes on low.

Spoon the sauce over the chicken breasts.

This dish works well when served over wide egg noodles or garlic mashies.

JUICY JADE CHICKEN

Serves 4

Ingredients

8 boneless, skinless chicken thighs

¼ cup dry sherry

¼ cup vegetable oil

1 red jalapeno chili, sliced thin

2 tbsp chili garlic sauce

2 tsp sesame oil

1 cup fresh mint leaves

2 tbsp soy sauce

4 tsp cornstarch

Preparation

Make the marinade first by combining the soy sauce and cornstarch in a medium sized bowl. Add the chicken pieces and thoroughly mix.

In a large frying pan or wok, heat the vegetable oil to high and brisky cook half the mint leaves for no more than 30 seconds. Remove and set aside.

Using the same pan or wok, add the chicken pieces and the jalapeno chili. Stir-fry aggressively for 3-4 minutes before adding the chili garlic sauce and sherry.

Introduce the sesame oil and the mint you previously cooked.

Plate the chicken and garnish with the remaining mint leaves.

This dish can either be an appetizer or served over Jasmine rice as an entrée.

KOREAN TERIYAKI CHICKEN

Serves 2

Ingredients

6 chicken breast tenders, cubed

1 medium onion, thinly sliced

1 sweet red pepper in olive oil, diced

1 package saffron rice

2 tbsp chili oil

⅓ cup Korean Teriyaki sauce (House of Tsang™)

Preparation

Prepare rice per package instructions.

Sauté chicken in chili oil over medium.

Add onion and red pepper when the chicken is nearly complete.

Introduce Korean Teriyaki sauce and cook for 3-5 minutes.

Serve over rice.

LEBANESE SHAWARMA CHICKEN

Serves 4

Ingredients

4 boneless, skinless chicken breasts

½ cup distilled vinegar

3 large lemons

4 cardamon pods

¼ tsp salt

¼ tsp pepper

Cooking spray

Preparation

Cut the chicken breasts into long, narrow strips. The easiest way to accomplish this is with a very sharp knife when the chicken is still semi-frozen.

Thoroughly mix the juice of three large lemons, vinegar, cardamon pods, salt and pepper.

Place the chicken in a deep dish and pour the juice mixture over them. Add just enough warm water to cover the chicken. Cover the dish with aluminum foil and leave in the fridge overnight to marinate.

Preheat oven to 350 degrees. Lightly spray a baking dish with cooking spray.

Place the chicken on the baking dish and cook for approximately 20 minutes, frequently turning.

ORANGE CHICKEN

Serves 4

Ingredients

2 boneless, skinless chicken breasts cut into 1-inch pieces

2 eggs

2 tbsp chopped garlic

⅔ cup orange juice (no pulp!)

¼ cup fresh squeezed lemon juice

2 tbsp hoisin sauce

2 tbsp sweet chili sauce

2 tbsp soy sauce

1 tbsp brown sugar

½ tsp red pepper flakes

½ tsp ginger, finely chopped

1 tbsp apple cider vinegar

¼ cup flour

½ cup cornstarch

Cooking oil for frying

White rice prepared per package instructions

2 scallions, thinly sliced, for finishing garnish

Preparation

In one bowl, beat the eggs. In a second bowl, mix the flour and cornstarch.

Coat the chicken pieces in the eggs first and then into the flour.

Heat enough oil in a large frying pan so it fills the bottom ¼ inch of the pan. Heat to medium.

Fry the chicken pieces for 4-5 minutes each and remove to paper towels to drain.

Serve with white rice.

PARMESAN CRUSTED CHICKEN

This dish is so ridiculously easy, you could practically make it in your sleep.

Serves 4

Ingredients

4 chicken breasts

½ cup mayonnaise

½ cup Parmesan cheese (grated)

4 tbsp Italian breadcrumbs

Preparation

Preheat oven to 425 degrees.

Fold the Parmesan cheese into the mayonnaise.

Place the chicken breasts on a baking sheet and use a pastry brush to coat the chicken with the cheese and mayonnaise mixture.

Sprinkle breadcrumbs over the top.

Bake for 22 minutes.

Serve with a green salad and wine.

PESTO CHICKEN IN PUFF PASTRY

You can make the pastry from scratch if you really want to. But if you're looking to save time and labor, you can buy it ready-made in the grocery store.

Serves 4

Ingredients

4 boneless, skinless chicken breasts

12 oz sheet of puff pastry

12 oz cherry tomatoes, halved

12 oz fresh green beans (ends snipped off)

4 tsp pesto

2 tbsp olive oil

¼ tsp salt

¼ tsp pepper

½ tsp garlic powder

Preparation

Pound the chicken to ½ in thickness.

Lay out the sheet of pastry dough. Cut in half horizontally, then cut vertically into 8 equal strips. This will yield 16 short strips.

Preheat oven to 425 degrees.

Season the chicken breasts with the salt and pepper and place in a roasting pan.

Lay four strips of pastry dough over each chicken breast and tuck in the ends. Using a pastry brush, paint each dough-encased chicken breast with half of the olive oil. Brush pesto over the top of each chicken breast.

In a smaller oven-proof pan, brush the rest of the olive oil over the cherry tomato halves and sprinkle with garlic powder.

Place both pans in the oven for 20 minutes.

While the chicken and tomatoes are baking, cook the green beans in boiling salt water until tender (6-7 minutes). Drain and set aside for garnish.

Plate the chicken and garnish with the tomatoes and green beans.

PROVENCE CHICKEN IN MUSTARD SAUCE

Serves 4

Ingredients

8 skinless, boneless chicken thighs

⅔ cup heavy whipping cream

½ cup yellow onion, diced

⅔ cup dry white wine

⅔ cup apple juice

2 tbsp butter

1 tbsp Dijon mustard

½ tsp Herbs de Provence

½ tsp ground ginger

½ tsp garlic powder

¼ tsp salt

¼ tsp pepper

4 small red apples, thinly sliced

Preparation

In a small bowl, mix the white wine, apple juice, Dijon, Herbs de Provence, garlic powder, and ginger.

In a large skillet, melt the butter and brown the chicken thighs on medium, 3 minutes each side.

Sprinkle the chicken thighs with salt and pepper, then add the diced onion and sliced apple.

Take the mixture you made in the small bowl and pour this over the top of the chicken.

Cover and reduce the heat to simmer. Simmer for 20-25 minutes.

Take out the chicken, onion and apple and put on a separate plate.

Bring the cooking liquid to a boil for about 3 minutes. Reduce the heat and pour in the heavy whipping cream, stirring until the mixture thickens.

Plate the chicken, apple and onion and generously pour the cream sauce over it.

ROASTED CHICKEN WITH SOUR CHERRIES

Serves 2

Ingredients

2 large boneless, skinless chicken breasts

1 cup chicken stock

¼ tsp salt

¼ tsp pepper

1 tbsp olive oil

½ cup black currant liquer (Cassis)

1 cup sour cherries, pitted

Preparation

Season the chicken breasts with the salt and pepper.

Preheat oven to 400 degrees.

In an oven-proof frying pan, heat the oil to medium-high.

Cook the chicken breasts for two minutes per side.

Place the frying pan in the oven and bake the chicken for 10 minutes. Remove the chicken breasts to a separate plate and keep warm.

In the same pan, introduce the chicken stock and the black currant liquer. Stirring constantly, cook over medium until your liquid has been reduced by half.

Add the cherries to the remaining liquid and simmer for 1-2 minutes.

Plate the chicken breasts and pour the cherry sauce over them.

TAILGATE TURKEY CHILI

Great for Game Night or just to take off a winter chill.

Serves 6

Ingredients

3 cups cooked turkey breast (cubed)

1 can rinsed and drained kidney beans

1 can rinsed and drained cannellini beans

1 can crushed tomatoes

1 can pumpkin

1 can chicken broth

⅔ cup sweet onion (chopped)

¼ cup green pepper (chopped)

¼ cup red pepper (chopped)

2 tbsp minced garlic

2 tbsp chili powder

2 tbsp brown sugar

2 tsp dried oregano

1 tsp ground cumin

½ tsp red pepper flakes

2 tbsp olive oil

1 cup shredded Mexican cheese

Preparation

In a large saucepan, sauté the onion, peppers, garlic, oregano and cumin in olive oil until fragrant.

Introduce the beans, tomatoes, chicken broth, pumpkin, brown sugar, chili powder, pepper flakes and half a cup of warm water.

Bring everything to a boil and then simmer, covered, for an hour.

Add the turkey last and heat until warmed through.

Top with the shredded Mexican cheese.

TANDOORI CHICKEN

Serves 4

Ingredients

4 boneless, skinless chicken breasts

1 large can of chickpeas, drained

3 cups Yukon gold potatoes, cubed

2 tbsp olive oil

2 tsp turmeric

2 tsp coriander

2 tsp cayenne

2 tsp cumin

2 tsp ground ginger

2 tsp curry powder

2 tsp chili powder

2 tsp paprika

½ tsp salt

½ tsp pepper

Preparation

Preheat oven to 375 degrees.

Line two baking sheets with parchment paper.

In a large bowl, mix all of the spices, salt and pepper. Season the chicken breasts with this mixture and place on one of the baking sheets. Drizzle 1 tbsp of olive oil over the chicken.

Spread the potatoes and the chickpeas out on the second baking sheet. Sprinkle with whatever herbs are left from the chicken and drizzle with the remaining tbsp of olive oil.

Bake for 20-25 minutes, turning the chicken over at the halfway point and, using a spatula, flip around the potatoes and chickpeas.

Combine everything in a large serving bowl for guests to serve themselves.

TURKEY BREASTS WITH ANCHOVY BUTTER

Serves 4

Ingredients

4 thinly sliced turkey breasts (I recommend having the butcher do this for you)

½ cup flour

1 cup dry white wine

3 tbsp olive oil

3 tbsp unsalted butter

2 small shallots (finely chopped)

2 tsp anchovy paste

2 tbsp dried chives

¼ tsp salt

¼ tsp pepper

Preparation

Mix the flour, salt and pepper. Dredge the turkey breasts in the flour, shaking off the excess.

Heat the oil in a large skillet on medium. Sauté the turkey breasts on each side until light golden brown. Remove from the frying pan to a plate and cover tightly with aluminum foil.

In the same pan where you did the turkey breasts, sauté the chopped shallots. Add the white wine and bring to a vigorous boil until the wine has reduced approximately by half.

On low heat, introduce the whisked anchovy paste, butter and chives. Return the turkey breasts to the skillet and allow them to be coated by the anchovy butter mixture prior to serving.

I recommend serving with peas, mashed potatoes and traditional stuffing. Christina and I often used this recipe to create "Thanksgiving in Summer," given that we had so much to be thankful in each other.

TURKEY CURRY

Serves 4

Ingredients

3 cups cooked turkey (shredded)

1 cup coconut milk

1½ cups chicken broth

3 carrots, thinly sliced

1 yellow onion, chopped

1 package frozen cauliflower (thaw out prior to cooking)

3 tbsp minced garlic

2 tbsp curry powder

2 tbsp fresh cilantro, minced

½ tsp salt

½ tsp pepper

½ tsp ground cardamom

1 cup commercial mango chutney

2 tsp flour

4 cups hot cooked rice

Preparation

In a large saucepan, combine the chicken broth, garlic and spices. Introduce the onions and carrots and bring to a boil.

Reduce the heat, add the thawed cauliflower and simmer for about 6 minutes.

Add the shredded turkey and chutney. While these are simmering on low, use a small mix bowl to mix the coconut milk and flour, stirring until smooth.

Pour this into the turkey and vegetables. Turn up the heat and continue to stir until the sauce has thickened.

Serve over rice.

TURKEY PESTO PASTA

You can also make this dish with shredded chicken.

Serves 4

Ingredients

2 cups cooked, shredded turkey

16 oz wide egg noodles

12 oz frozen peas

1 cup basil pesto (easily purchased at the store)

½ cup heavy whipping cream

1 jar sun-dried tomatoes, drained

1 cup shredded Mozzarella

Cooking spray

Preparation

Boil the egg noodles per package instructions. Drain and mix in the turkey, cream, pesto, sun-dried tomatoes and frozen peas.

Preheat oven to 400 degrees. Spray the bottom and interior sides of a 9x13 inch baking dish.

Pour the pasta and turkey mixture into the baking dish.

Generously sprinkle the Mozzarella over the top.

Bake for 20 minutes until the cheese has melted and is bubbly.

TURKEY TETRAZINNI

Wondering what to do with that leftover turkey? This will get you started.

Serves 4

Ingredients

1 lb cooked turkey (shredded)

1 package (16 oz) wide egg noodles

⅔ cup yellow onion (chopped)

2 cups whole milk

¼ cup butter

¼ cup flour

½ cup grated Gruyere

½ cup grated Cheddar

½ teaspoon poultry seasoning

1 tsp salt

¼ tsp pepper

¼ teaspoon ground mustard

1 (4.5 oz) can sliced mushrooms

Cooking spray

Preparation

Bring the egg noodles to boil in a large pot. Cook for 5 minutes. Drain and remove from heat.

In a medium saucepan, sauté the onion in butter. Add the flour, followed by the milk and stir until the lumps dissolve. Introduce the seasonings and mustard and mix. Add half the cheese (1/4 cup Gruyere and ¼ cup Cheddar). Lastly, add the drained mushrooms.

Preheat oven to 400 degrees and use cooking spray on the bottom and sides of your 9x13 inch baking dish.

Place a layer of egg noodles on the bottom followed by a layer of turkey and cheese sauce. Repeat until you have used everything up. Top with the remaining Gruyere and Cheddar.

Bake for 25 minutes until the top is bubbly and golden.

TURMERIC CHICKEN

Serves 4

Ingredients

8 boneless, skinless chicken thighs, cut into bite-sized pieces

1 medium yellow onion, chopped

4 tbsp minced garlic

3 tbsp butter

3 plum tomatoes, chopped

3 cups chicken stock

2 tsp ground turmeric

2 tsp curry powder

2 tbsp butter

1 tbsp finely chopped ginger

½ tsp ground cumin

½ tsp cinnamon

2 tbsp fish sauce

2 cups uncooked white or Jasmine rice

¼ tsp salt

¼ tsp black pepper

Preparation

Sprinkle the salt and pepper over the chicken thighs.

In a large casserole dish on the stovetop, melt the butter and add the turmeric, stirring until mixed.

Add the chicken thighs and cook over medium, four minutes per side. Remove to a separate plate.

In the same pan, sauté the chopped onion, minced garlic and chopped ginger for 3-4 minutes. It will smell fabulously fragrant!

Next, introduce the tomatoes, curry powder, cumin and cinnamon. Add the uncooked rice and continue to stir.

Return the chicken thighs to the casserole dish, along with the chicken stock and fish sauce.

Cover the casserole dish and simmer on low heat for 10-15 minutes. Partially cover the casserole contents and heat for an additional 10-15 minutes (still on low) to ensure the rich has cooked through.

TUSCANY CHICKEN BREASTS

Serves 4

Ingredients

4 boneless, skinless chicken breasts

¾ cup heavy whipping cream

1 bag baby spinach

4 tbsp butter

1 tbsp olive oil

¼ tsp salt

¼ tsp pepper

1 cup cherry tomatoes, halved

4 tbsp minced garlic

1 tsp dried oregano

½ cup grated Parmesan

Preparation

In a large frying pan, heat the olive oil to medium.

Rub the salt, pepper and oregano into the chicken breasts.

Fry the chicken on both sides of 7-8 minutes. Remove to a separate plate and keep warm.

Using the same pan, melt the butter. Stir in the garlic and cherry tomatoes for 2-3 minutes. Turn down the heat and add the baby spinach.

The moment the baby spinach starts to melt (and believe me, it will do this quickly!), pour in the heavy whipping cream and the grated Parmesan. Simmer on low for 2-3 minutes.

Bring the chicken breasts back to the frying pan and cook for an additional 5-7 minutes.

MEATS

Meats work their way into the main courses of virtually all foods across the globe. Whether beef, lamb, pork, or more exotic fare is on the menu, meats can be served at any time of the day and in a wide range of healthy, and not so healthy, forms. Whether grilled or slow-roasted to perfection as a signature dish, shredded or thinly sliced for use in main courses anywhere from Latin America to the Far East, or ground for sandwiches, meatballs, or filling for empanadas or pot stickers, there is a near endless variety of ways in which meats are used in cooking.

Meats and fowl lend themselves to marinades and dry rubs. For many, however, especially for those using a grill, the key is time and temperature and a modest amount of sea salt and cracked black pepper. Certainly, nothing wrong with that, especially when grilling at high or very high heat. Roasting meats, whether a beef or pork tenderloin or a lamb shank, provides the opportunity to integrate herbs and spices, wine, vegetables or mushrooms into the cooking process. These additions allow the meat flavor to influence the other food in the pan and in turn allowing the vegetables or other items to impart their flavor to the meat and the sauce or gravy that results from slow cooking meat.

If you want to expand your culinary horizons while maintaining the sanctity of the grill, consider looking at cookbooks from throughout the globe and see how grilled meats are prepared. One of my favorite adds to a grilled steak is anchovy paste. The normal reaction to that comment is, "Seriously?" Except when I mention it to someone who knows the cooking of Provence. Anchovy paste rubbed into a beef steak, before the obligatory salt and pepper, adds remarkable depth to the meat. Consider Jamaican jerk marinates for chicken or an Italian salad dressing before grilling. Note, that if using lemon, vinegar, or other highly acidic liquids for a marinade, reduce the time appropriately. These acids will start the cooking process.

Marinades and rubs should complement the meat and not overwhelm it. If grilling at high heat, dry rubs with herbs may not be the best idea as they may burn while the meat is cooking. Conversely, herbs are well suited to roasting, but remember that whatever marinade you use for a roast will infuse itself into everything else that is in the pan. As is always the case, let your nose be your guide.

As I indicated earlier, we do very little grilling, particularly outdoors on a high temperature grill. For those who do, bravo!

A MEAT LOAF BY ANY OTHER NAME

Meat loaf. Yes, really. Meat loaf. Ordinary. Simple. Pedestrian. If you served it on a paper plate with a plastic fork, your dinner guest would likely not be impressed. But what if you called it "Polpettone," "Pain de Viande," "Bolo de Carne" or "Köttfärslimpa" and plated it on your best China with crisp linen napkins, sterling silver and an amusing wine? Appreciation of gourmet cuisine is sometimes just a matter of what you call your entrée and how you present it.

Serves 4

Ingredients

¾ lb ground beef

¾ lb ground pork

2 large eggs

1 cup Italian breadcrumbs

1 medium yellow onion (diced)

1 tbsp minced garlic

½ cup ketchup

2 tsp brown sugar

2 tbsp fresh parsley (finely chopped)

1 tbsp Worcestershire sauce

4 strips uncooked bacon cut in half

Non-stick cooking spray

Preparation

Preheat oven to 350 degrees. Spray the bottom and sides of a 9x5 inch loaf pan.

Mix all of the ingredients with the exception of the bacon strips, brown sugar, ¼ cup of ketchup, and Worcestershire sauce.

Fill the loaf pan with the meatloaf mixture.

Lay the uncooked strips of bacon in one-layer stripes across the top and tuck in the ends.

Bake for 30 minutes. In the meantime, whisk together the remainder of the ketchup, brown sugar and Worcestershire sauce in a small bowl.

Remove the meat loaf and, using a pastry brush, coat the top of the loaf with the ketchup mixture. Return to the oven for an additional 20-25 minutes or until the top has formed a glaze.

Allow to rest 10 minutes prior to slicing.

BAKED PORK LOIN

Serves 4

Ingredients

4 center-cut pork loin

1 russet potato

1 cup chopped yellow onion

6 oz grated Gruyere

6 oz ricotta

2 tbsp mayonnaise

2 tbsp Dijon mustard

2 tbsp olive oil

Cooking spray

Preparation

Peel and grate the potato.

In a medium bowl, combine the Gruyere, ricotta, mayonnaise and mustard.

Preheat oven to 375 degrees.

Spray the bottom and interior sides of a casserole dish. Place the grated potato on the bottom.

This is followed by a layer of chopped onion.

Place the pork on top of the onion. Spoon the cheese, ricotta, mayonnaise and mustard over the top of the pork

Drizzle the olive oil over the pork and cover the entire thing with aluminum foil.

Bake for 20 minutes.

BEEF BOURGUIGNON

It's a labor-intensive dish for sure but it not only smells fabulous while it's cooking, it also makes for great leftovers during the week. The secret is to allow the beef to marinate in the refrigerator for 2 full days prior to cooking.

Serves 4

Ingredients

2 lbs of beef chuck roast (cubed to bite-size)

3 cups red wine (Cabernet Sauvignon or Zinfandel work well)

2 medium onions (diced)

2 carrots (peeled and finely sliced)

2 tbsp garlic (minced)

1 tsp salt

1 tsp pepper

2 tbsp brandy

4 tbsp olive oil

4 tbsp butter

4 strips bacon (sliced in 1-inch pieces)

1 can commercial beef broth

1 cup white mushrooms (thinly sliced)

Cooking spray

Preparation

In a large lidded bowl, combine the beef, red wine, carrots, half the onion, garlic, brandy, salt and pepper. Marinate in the fridge for 2 days.

In a large skillet, heat 2 tbsp of olive oil. Use a slotted spoon to transfer the beef and vegetables (but don't toss the remaining marinade.)

Sauté until the beef is nicely browned. Remove to a separate bowl.

Using the same skillet, brown the bacon. Add the bacon to the beef and vegetables. Using the same skillet, add the remaining olive oil, butter, onions, beef broth, sliced mushrooms and the rest of the marinade. Heat on medium for approximately 2 minutes. Add this to the beef and vegetables.

Preheat oven to 300 degrees. Spray a large casserole dish. Spoon the meat and vegetable mixture into the casserole dish and heat for 2-3 hours until the beef is completely tender. If needed, add additional splashes of wine to keep everything moist.

BRILLIANT BASIL BEEF

Serves 4

Ingredients

1 lb flank steak, cut into narrow strips (do this while the meat is still semi-frozen)

1 jalapeno chili, sliced very thin

2 shallots, thinly sliced

1 tbsp olive oil

¾ cup fresh basil leaves

1 tbsp soy sauce

1 tbsp cornstarch

Preparation

Make the marinade first in a medium sided bowl by thoroughly combining the soy sauce and cornstarch. Add the strips of beef and ensure they all get a nice dunking in the marinade. Let stand at room temperature for 15-20 minutes.

In a large skillet or wok, heat the oil on high.

Sauté the shallots and the chili for about 30 seconds. Reduce the heat and add the marinated beef, stirring constantly for about 5 minutes.

Plate the beef and top with the basil leaves. (The heat of the beef will happily wilt these.)

FLAWLESS SPAGHETTI SAUCE

Serves 4

Ingredients

½ lb ground beef

½ lb ground Italian sausage or ground pork

1 medium yellow onion, chopped

15 oz tomato sauce

6 oz tomato paste

1 tsp garlic powder

1 tsp Italian seasoning

1 tsp crushed red pepper flakes

1 tbsp chopped fresh parsley

1 tbsp sugar

1 tbsp Worcestershire sauce

1 tbsp olive oil

½ cup fresh chopped basil

Preparation

In a large skillet, heat the olive oil and brown the meat along with the chopped onion.

Drain the excess grease but leave the meat and onion in the skillet.

Add the tomato sauce, tomato paste, all of the herbs, Worcestershire sauce, parsley and sugar.

Add a cup of warm water and bring to a boil.

Reduce the heat and simmer uncovered for 30-35 minutes.

Add the fresh basil just prior to serving.

HOLIDAY PORK TENDERLOIN

If it is just a table for two this season, here is a flavorful suggestion using pork tenderloin that has the evocative taste of the holidays without the leftovers!

Ingredients

Pork:

1 lb. pork tenderloin

Commercial pork rub (my preference is *Rub With Love* by Tom Douglas)

Salt and pepper

½ tbsp salted butter

1 tbsp olive oil

1 cup prepared veal stock with a splash of sherry

Carrots:

12 oz baby carrots

2 tbsp lavender infused extra virgin olive oil

¼ cup lavender honey

2 tbsp Herbs de Provence

Salt and ground green pepper

Sauce:

1 shallot, finely chopped

2 cloves of chopped garlic

2 tbsp salted butter

1 pint of prepared veal stock

¼ cup ruby port

¼ cup heavy cream

Cornstarch

1 cup sliced baby Portobello mushrooms

Black pepper to taste

Commercial stove-top stuffing

Preparation

Preheat the oven to 350 degrees.

Sprinkle salt and pepper over the tenderloin and then coal lightly with a commercial pork rub. On the stove top, melt the butter and olive oil on medium heat, then brown the tenderloin on all sides. Turn heat to low.

Add half of the veal stock/sherry mix, cover, and place in the oven. Set the time for 35 minutes, and place in oven.

Next, line a baking sheet with aluminum foil. Place the baby carrots on the sheet. Drizzle with the olive oil and honey and evenly sprinkle the Herbs de Provence, salt and pepper over the carrots.

When the timer goes off, turn the pork over, add the rest of the veal stock/sherry mix and return to oven. Set the timer for 10 minutes. When the timer goes off, place the carrots in the oven and set the timer for an additional 20 minutes. Turn the carrots after 10 minutes.

With about 10 minutes left for the pork and carrots to cook, in a large pan prepare the stuffing per directions on the package. In a sauce pan, sauté the shallot and garlic in the butter on medium heat until fragrant. Add cornstarch and heavy cream and stir until the roux thickens. Add the veal stock, port, and mushrooms and stir under low heat as the gravy thickens. If needed, add additional cornstarch stirred in hot water to thicken the gravy.

When the pork is done, remove from oven and wrap in foil. Allow to rest for 10 minutes. After rested, remove the carrots from the oven.

Slice the tenderloin into medallions, serve with carrots and dressing, spoon sauce over the pork and reserve the rest for use at the table.

CHRISTINA'S MEXICAN LASAGNA

Serves 4

Ingredients

2 tbsp oil

½ cup medium yellow onion, chopped

1 lb. ground beef

1 tbsp chili powder

1 (19-oz) can of red enchilada sauce

1 small can of sliced black olives

¾ tbsp. finely chopped cilantro

No-boil flat, wide lasagna (I recommend Barilla™)

1 pkg grated 4-cheese Mexican blend

Preparation

In a large frying pan, brown the chopped onion and ground beef in the cooking oil. Add the chili powder, enchilada sauce, olives and cilantro and simmer on low for about 15 minutes. Remove from heat, cover and allow to cool down.

Spray an 8-inch square Pyrex dish with nonstick cooking spray. Place two of the pieces of lasagna side-by-side in the bottom of the dish. Using a large spoon, cover the lasagna with a generous layer of the meat sauce. Top this layer with a generous sprinkle of grated cheese. On top of the cheese, place two more pieces of lasagna and repeat the meat and cheese layers. You will have enough to create three layers that almost reach the top of the dish. Preheat oven to 350 degrees. Cover dish with aluminum foil and bake for 45 minutes. Remove the foil, lower heat to 300 degrees and bake for an additional 20 minutes.

Serve with a salad and red wine.

MOORISH PORK KABOBS

Serves 4

Ingredients

1 lb pork, cubed

2 tbsp minced garlic

1 tsp curry powder (mild or hot, depending on your pref)

1 tsp Spanish paprika

½ tsp coriander seeds

¼ tsp thyme (dried)

¼ tsp black pepper

Preparation

Blend the garlic, curry powder, paprika, coriander and pepper.

Put 4-5 pieces of cubed pork on a metal skewer and thoroughly coat with the dry mixture you just made.

Allow to rest in the fridge for about 3 hours.

Placed the skewered pork on foil under an oven broiler or atop a hot barbecue and cook for about 3 minutes on each side.

Serve with a rice pilaf or salad.

MOROCCAN LAMB AND PATATAS BRAVAS

Serves 2-4

Ingredients

2 medium russet potatoes

1 lb. ground lamb (ground beef can be substituted)

⅓ cup minced garlic

2 tbsp Spanish Rub (prepared in advance)

2 tbsp olive oil

Feta cheese crumbled (optional)

Chopped parsley

Harissa (optional)

Pita Bread (optional)

Spanish Rub:

1 tbsp. hot pimentón

1 tsp. coriander

1 tsp. turmeric

1 tsp. white pepper

½ tsp. cumin

½ tsp. garlic powder

Pinch of salt

Preparation

Peel potatoes and parboil for 10 minutes. Once cooled, quarter lengthwise (halve and halve again) and then cut crosswise in about ½ inch wedges.

Heat olive oil to medium (water droplet bubbles up when splashed) and add potatoes.

Brown lamb and break into crumbles. Add garlic while browning. As the meat begins to separate and cook, add Spanish Rub and coat meat evenly. Potatoes are done once they begin to lightly brown on the surface.

Serving

Using a slotted spoon, place potatoes paper towels to absorb extra oil. Place potatoes on plate. Spoon lamb over potatoes. Top with crumbled feta cheese (optional). Top with finely chopped parsley.

Harissa (hot Moroccan chili paste) on the side. Use pita bread to put mixture on if you like.

MUSTARD PORK CHOPS WITH APPLES

Serves 4

Ingredients

4 pork chops

1 medium onion (thinly sliced)

2 medium red apples (thinly sliced)

2 tbsp olive oil

½ cup chicken broth

½ tsp salt

½ tsp pepper

1 cup heavy whipping cream

⅓ cup Dijon mustard

3 tbsp bourbon

Preparation

Preheat oven to 425 degrees.

In a large frying pan, heat the olive oil to medium. Rub salt and pepper on the pork chops and heat for 5 minutes per side. Remove to a separate plate and keep warm.

In the same frying pan, brown the apple and onion slices. Remove these to a separate plate as well.

Pour the broth into the skillet and stir constantly to scrape up the sticky bits at the bottom. Add the chicken broth, heavy whipping cream and mustard and simmer until this mixture starts to bubble.

Temporarily remove the skillet from the heat so you can add the bourbon. (Do not add the bourbon while the pan is on the stove.)

Place the pork chops in the sauce and top with the apples and onions. Put the frying pan in the oven for 10-12 minutes or until the sauce bubbles. Remove for serving.

PORK CHIMICHANGAS

This recipe can also be made with shredded beef, chicken, turkey or even shrimp.

Serves 2-4

Ingredients

2 cups shredded, cooked pork

1 cup Mexican cheese blend, grated

½ cup sour cream

½ cup commercial salsa

½ cup black beans (drained and rinsed)

½ cup green chilies (diced)

½ tsp garlic powder

½ tsp onion powder

½ tsp smoked paprika

1 tsp ground cumin

4 large flour tortillas

2 tbsp olive oil

Cooking spray

Preparation

Preheat oven to 400 degrees and prep a baking sheet with cooking spray.

In a large bowl, combine the pork, cheese, sour cream, salsa, black beans, green chilies and spices. Mix thoroughly.

Place each tortilla flat on a cutting board and put the above mixture in the center. Roll the tortillas up and tuck in the outer ends.

Use a pastry brush to generously coat each chimichanga with olive oil.

Place each chimichanga on the baking sheet with the seam side facing down.

Bake for 20-25 minutes or until the outer surface of the tortilla is crispy and golden.

Serve with a generous dollop of sour cream, guacamole or salsa.

RAGIN' CAJUN BEEF SIRLOIN

Serves 4

Ingredients

1½ lb beef sirloin

½ cup sliced cremini mushrooms

½ cup sliced white mushrooms

1 small yellow onion, sliced

2 tbsp Cajun seasoning (I recommend Slap Ya Mama™)

2 tbsp olive oil

2 tbsp butter

1 tbsp minced garlic

2 cups dry red wine

Preparation

Thoroughly rub the piece of beef with Cajun seasoning and allow to rest at room temperature for 10 minutes.

In a large frying pan, heat the olive oil to medium and brown the beef (approximately 7 minutes per side). Remove to a separate platter and keep warm.

In the same frying pan, melt the butter and sauté the mushrooms, onion and garlic.

Introduce the wine and bring to a boil. Continue stirring until the liquid is reduced to half.

Slice the beef into strips, plate, and serve the sauce over it.

ROAST HAWAIIAN PORK

If a trip to the Hawaiian Islands for a luau isn't in the budget, here's an easy version of roast Hawaiian pork you can make in your own oven.

Serves 6-8

Ingredients

4 lb pork shoulder

1 cup soy sauce

1 cup brown sugar

2 tbsp minced ginger

½ cup mirin

Preparation

Heat all of the marinade ingredients on the stovetop on medium, whisking briskly. Remove from stove and allow to cool before putting in a lidded container for storage in the refrigerator. This can be made up to a full day prior to use.

Make shallow diagonal cuts along the surface of the pork to allow the marinade to enter. Marinate the pork shoulder overnight in the Hawaiian marinade.

Preheat oven to 350 degrees.

In a large roasting pan, lay down a large piece of aluminum foil and, on top of that, a large piece of parchment. Bring all four sides of both the parchment and the aluminum foil over the pork shoulder and tightly seal it into its own cocoon.

Heat for one hour. Reduce the heat to 325 degrees and, with the pork still wrapped up, bake for an additional three hours.

Upon finally removing the pork from the oven, allow to rest for 15 minutes before unwrapping the foil. There will be lots of steam coming out so just make sure you're not standing directly over it.

Use forks to shred the succulent finished product.

SHANGHAI'D MEATBALLS

The meatballs can be made ahead of time, stored in the fridge and then brought out when

you're ready to introduce them to the other ingredients.

Serves 2-4

Ingredients

1 lb ground pork

2-½ tbsp finely chopped green onion

1 tsp grated ginger

1 tsp salt

1 tbsp Chinese five spice

2 tbsp dry sherry

3-4 baby bok choy

Dash of garlic powder

Cooking oil

4 cups chicken broth

Preparation

Thoroughly mix the pork, green onion, Chinese five spice, ginger, salt and sherry. Form into eight large meatballs and set aside.

Chop the baby bok choy into 1-inch pieces. On low heat, lightly sauté the bok choy with garlic powder in a tiny smidge of cooking oil. It's important to note that, like spinach, bok choy is mostly liquid and cooks quite quickly. Thus, you should do only a light sauté to warm it up, not cook it down to a bunch of green nothingness.

Spread half the bok choy across the bottom of a deep casserole dish. Place the uncooked meatballs on top and cover with the remainder of the bok choy.

Add boiling chicken broth to just cover the meatballs. Cover the casserole and simmer on low heat for two hours.

SHEPHERD'S PIE

This quintessentially British comfort food is done with ground lamb. You can also use beef if you prefer, wherein it is called Cottage Pie. (Substitute beef stock for chicken stock.) It's also traditional to only do the mashed potatoes on top. My own spin is a layer of mashies on the bottom as well.

Serves 4

Ingredients

1½ lbs ground lamb

4 medium potatoes

1 stick of butter

1 medium onion (chopped)

1½ cups frozen mixed vegetables (I like peas, corn and carrots)

½ cup chicken broth

1 tsp Worcestershire sauce

1 tbsp garlic powder

1 tbsp sage

Non-stick cooking spray

Salt and pepper to taste

Preparation

Peel, quarter and par-boil the potatoes as if you were making mashies (which, actually, you are).

In a large frying pan, melt half the butter in which to sauté the chopped onion.

Add the (defrosted) vegetables and continue to sauté.

Introduce the ground lamb, chicken broth, garlic powder, sage, and Worcestershire sauce and stir continuously until the lamb is cooked. Lightly season with salt and pepper.

Mash the potatoes in a large bowl with the remaining butter.

In a large baking casserole dish, spray the bottom and sides with cooking spray. Spoon a generous layer of mashed potatoes on the bottom. Add the cooked lamb and vegetable filling and top the casserole with the rest of the mashed potatoes.

Bake in the oven at 375 degrees for 30-40 minutes until the top "crust" is nicely browned.

SPICY PEPPER STEAK

Serves 4

Ingredients

1 lb top round beef, sliced into thin strips (either have the butcher do this for you or slice the beef yourself when it is semi-frozen)

10 oz beef broth

1 cup chopped yellow onion

2 tbsp butter

2 tbsp minced garlic

1 green pepper, seeded and cut into strips

1 red bell pepper, seeded and cut into strips

2 Roma tomatoes cut into wedges

2 tbsp butter

2 tbsp cornstarch

1 tbsp smoked paprika

2 tbsp soy sauce

Preparation

Rub the smoked paprika into the meat strips.

Heat the butter in a large frying pan over medium. Brown the beef and onion. Add to this the minced garlic and beef broth. Cover and simmer on low for half an hour.

Introduce the green and red pepper strips. Stir. Cover and simmer for another 5 minutes.

Sprinkle in the cornstarch, soy sauce and about ½ cup of warm water. Once the sauce has thickened, add the tomato wedges. Serve over white rice or wide egg noodles.

SPICY SAUSAGE POTATO BOATS

Serves 4

Ingredients

4 medium russet potatoes

3 tbsp olive oil

1 tbsp butter

1 small yellow onion, diced

1-½ cup sausage

1 tsp garlic salt

1 tsp Cajun seasoning (Slap Ya Mama™ or Morton & Bassett Cajun Spice Blend™)

4 eggs

½ cup Gruyere

Instructions

Using a pastry brush, coat each of the potatoes with 1 tbsp of olive oil. Place on a baking sheet, cover tightly with aluminum foil and bake at 375 degrees for 35 minutes.

While the potatoes are cooking, heat 1 tbsp butter and 2 tbsp olive oil in a medium pan. Add the diced onion and sausage and sauté on medium until the sausage is cooked. Sprinkle in the garlic salt and Cajun seasoning and mix thoroughly. Feel free to add more Cajun seasoning if you like extra heat.

Remove the potatoes and, laying them lengthwise, cut off ⅓ from the right side of each. Using a spoon, scoop out the inside of each potato so an oval well is formed. Fill each well with the sausage mixture, then gently break an egg into each "boat." Top each one with Gruyere.

Bake uncovered in the oven at 350 degrees for 30 minutes.

Note: The potato you have scooped out can be saved for whipped potatoes. Just add butter, heavy whipping cream, light garlic powder and heat in a saucepan. Top with chives.

STUFFED FLANK STEAK

A surprisingly easy meal which always looks as if you went to much, much more work.

Serves 4

Ingredients

1½ lbs flank steak, pounded very thin (You may want to ask your butcher to do this for you)

2 cups Stove Top Stuffing™

½ cup red wine

1 red or green bell pepper, seeded and finely chopped

2 tbsp butter

2 tbsp minced garlic

2 green onions, finely chopped

1 cup beef broth

½ cup button mushrooms, thinly sliced

3 tbsp grated Parmesan

Cooking spray

Preparation

Combine the dry stuffing mix, 1 cup of boiling water and the butter in a mixing bowl.

After mixing, let it stand for 5-10 minutes, then spoon the dressing along the center of the flank steak. Sprinkle with the green onion and chopped bell pepper.

Roll up the steak and secure the open ends with toothpicks.

Preheat oven to 350 degrees.

Spray the bottom and interior sides of a 9x13 inch baking dish.

In a small bowl, mix the beef broth, wine, minced garlic, mushrooms and Parmesan cheese. Pour this liberally over the rolled up flank steak.

Bake for one hour. Allow to stand for 5-10 minutes before slicing.

SUNDAY POT ROAST

Serves 4 (+ leftovers!)

Ingredients

3 lb beef chuck pot roast

1 cup yellow onion (chopped)

1 cup baby carrots

1 cup celery (thinly sliced)

2 tbsp olive oil

1 tsp salt

1 tsp pepper

1 tsp dried rosemary

½ cup butter

Preparation

In a large, oven-safe pot, heat the olive oil.

Rub the salt and pepper all over the beef.

Brown on both sides in the olive oil and remove to a plate.

In the same pot, add the butter, onions, celery and carrots and sauté for 5-6 minutes.

Return the browned beef to the pot, sprinkle with the rosemary.

Preheat oven to 275 degrees.

Cover the cooking pot and place in oven. Bake for 2-3 hours.

Tip: If you're not a fan of celery, substitute with 1 cup of diced red potato.

SWEDISH MEATBALLS

Yes, there are dry-mix packets in the grocery store for whipping up Swedish meatballs if you're really in a hurry but they just don't taste as comforting as making it all from scratch.

Serves 4

Ingredients

1 lb ground beef

1 lb ground pork

2 eggs

1 medium yellow onion (chopped)

¾ cup seasoned breadcrumbs

½ tsp salt

½ tsp pepper

½ cup fresh chopped parsley

½ cup flour

2½ cups whole milk

32 oz beef broth

1 tbsp Worcestershire sauce

¼ tsp nutmeg

¼ tsp allspice

1 package wide egg noodles

4 tbsp butter

Preparation

In a large mixing bowl, thoroughly mix the beef, pork, onion, eggs, breadcrumbs, parsley, salt and pepper. Shape the meat into 1½ inch balls.

Brown the meatballs in a large frying pan over medium. Use a slotted spoon to remove them to a large plate of paper towels to drain.

Using the oily residue in the frying pan, stir in the flour, milk, beef broth, Worcestershire sauce, nutmeg and allspice. Over medium heat, bring this to a boil and stir until it thickens.

Reduce the heat to low and now add the meatballs to the sauce. Continue to cook for about 20 minutes, remembering to occasionally stir.

Prepare the egg noodles according to package instructions. Drain the pasta, toss with butter. Plate the pasta and serve the Swedish meatballs on top. If you like, garnish with additional parsley.

DESSERTS

How sweet it is! I love desserts. Whether in a restaurant or a home, there is something emphatic about a signature dessert at the end of a special meal. On the other hand, a simple sweet is always welcomed when the palette has been blessed by a savory or luxuriant main course and the admonition "make sure to save room for dessert" was blissfully left unheeded.

As is the case with all aspects of a meal, dessert requires the same thoughtfulness and preparation as every other course.

Desserts can fall into one of three basic categories: (1) homemade, (2) store bought, or (3) simple but effective. If you have a signature dessert you want to proudly present to family and friends—and you are also in charge of the rest of the menu—then take the time to build a meal around the dessert. Of course, all bets are off on holiday meals when over-indulgence is considered the norm. But for the rest of the year people do not necessarily want to be over-stuffed. In other words, if you want your family and guests to save room for dessert, fix a meal which makes that possible.

If you want a pie, cake, or tart to serve, then certainly there is no shortage of bakeries which can accommodate your delectable request. As is the case with every part of the meal, however, make sure that what you are serving is within the tolerances of your guests. That includes keeping a close eye on not only taste (while beautiful to present, not everyone loves kiwifruit) but also on allergies. This is especially the case with nut allergies.

On the other hand, if the meal rises and falls on the main course, then perhaps German Chocolate Cake or Coconut Cream Pie is not the best coda for your gastronomic symphony. Consider ice creams, gelatos, or sorbets—with or without fresh fruit—and teas or coffee to wind down the evening. Cookies, biscotti, baklava or shortbreads certainly fit into this category as well. Not only will you and your guests enjoy the sweets but it will take less effort to get up from the table when the meal is over!

CHOCA-RUMBA BALLS

Ingredients

⅓ cup dark rum

4 oz soft cream cheese

1 cup sugar

3 oz melted unsweetened chocolate

1 tsp instant coffee granules

¾ cup almonds, finely ground

8 Oreo cookies

Preparation

In a small bowl, pour the rum and dissolve the instant coffee granules into it.

Add the softened cream cheese, sugar and finely ground almonds to the rum and thoroughly blend.

Melt the chocolate in the microwave and pour this into the mixture. Mix well.

Cover and refrigerate for at least two hours.

Using a rolling pin, crush the Oreo cookies.

Shape your chocolate mixture into 1-inch balls and coat in the crushed Oreo cookies.

CHOCOLATE MOUSSE

Serves 2 (or 1 person who is very hungry and loves chocolate)

Ingredients

½ cup semi-sweet chocolate chips

½ cup heavy whipping cream

1 egg yolk, whisked

1 tbsp sugar

2 tsp vanilla extract

Whipped cream

2 sprigs of fresh mint

Preparation

Melt the chocolate chips in a small saucepan with a tablespoon of water.

Add the egg yolk and stir until the mixture starts to thicken. Stir in the vanilla extract.

Pour into a small bowl and allow to cool.

In a separate bowl, beat the whipping cream until it thickens. Add the sugar and beat until fluffy.

Fold the whipping cream and sugar into the chocolate and mix thoroughly. Distribute this mixture to the dessert bowls you plan to use and refrigerate for 2-3 hours.

Dollop with whipped cream and garnish with the sprigs of fresh mint.

FLOURLESS CHOCOLATE CAKE

Which of course, would be even better if it were calorie-less chocolate cake. Sigh.

Ingredients

6 eggs

1 oz bittersweet chocolate (pieces broken up)

1 cup butter

¾ cup sugar

½ cup water

Cooking spray

Preparation

In a medium saucepan, combine the sugar and water and stir until the sugar has dissolved.

Microwave the chocolate pieces to melt them. Pour this into a blender.

Lightly melt the butter and pour this into the chocolate in the blender.

Pour in the water, followed by the eggs.

Preheat the oven to 300 degrees and spray the bottom and interior sides of a cake pan.

Pour the batter into the cake pan.

Fill a slightly larger cake pan with boiling water which comes halfway up the outer sides of the first cake pan.

Bake for 45 minutes.

Put the cake in the fridge and allow it to chill. This generally takes overnight.

To make for an easy release of the cake from the cake pan, dip the bottom of the cake pan in hot water for about 15 seconds.

Invert onto a plate. Voila!

LEMON CHEESECAKE

Ingredients

1 graham cracker crust (unless you love making crusts, save time and just buy one at the store)

3 eggs

32 oz softened cream cheese

½ cup fresh squeezed lemon juice

1 tbsp lemon zest

⅓ cup sour cream

1¼ cups sugar

1 tsp vanilla extract

Preparation

In a small bowl, thoroughly blend the sugar and lemon zest.

Pour this into a blender and add the softened cream cheese, lemon juice, sour cream and vanilla extract.

Add the eggs, one at a time, and blend until creamy.

Pour this into the graham cracker crust.

Preheat oven to 350 degrees.

Boil a large pan of water (about 1 inch deep) and place on the rack directly below the cheesecake.

Bake uncovered for 55-60 minutes.

Remove from oven and cool for an hour.

Serve with a topping of whipped cream, lemon curd or fresh berries.

MEXICAN PUDDING CAKE

Ingredients

1 cup flour

½ cup brown sugar

½ cup white sugar

½ cup milk

3 tbsp dark cocoa

2 tsp baking powder

¾ tsp cinnamon

1 tsp vanilla extract

¼ tsp salt

¼ tsp cayenne

2 tbsp oil

Cooking spray

Ingredients to top it off:

½ cup brown sugar

½ cup white sugar

2 tbsp dark cocoa

1 cup milk

1 tsp espresso powder

Preparation

Mix the topping first by combining all of the ingredients in a small bowl.

In a large bowl, combine the flour, sugars, cocoa, salt, cinnamon and cayenne.

In a small bowl, mix the oil with the vanilla and milk. Pour this into the larger bowl of dry ingredients and thoroughly mix.

Preheat the oven to 375 degrees. Use cooking spray on the bottom and interior sides of your cake pan. Pour the batter into the pan. Next, pour your topping mixture over the cake and spread evenly.

Bake for 40 minutes. Remove to rest and cool prior to slicing.

MINT CHIP CHOCOLATE COOKIES

These are Christina's favorite.

Ingredients

2½ cups flour

1½ cups mint chocolate chips

1 tsp baking soda

1½ tsp cornstarch

1 cup melted butter

½ tsp salt

¾ cup brown sugar

½ cup white sugar

2 tsp vanilla extract

1 egg

1 egg yolk

Preparation

In a large mixing bowl, mix together the flour, cornstarch, baking soda and salt.

In a separate bowl, mix the melted butter and both sugars. Introduce the egg and the egg yolk. Whisk thoroughly. Add the vanilla extract.

Fold this into the large bowl of dry ingredients. Lastly, add the mint chips.

Cover the bowl tightly and chill overnight in the refrigerator.

On the day of baking, preheat the oven to 325 degrees. This will allow time for the cookie dough to come to room temperature.

Line your baking sheets with parchment paper.

Roll the cookie dough into small balls and slightly flatten.

Bake for 12-14 minutes. Remove to cooling rack.

WINING WITH DINING

A lot of people admit to confusion when it comes to pairing wines with food and understanding what kind of vino to order in a restaurant. They know wine derives from grapes and that they should drink reds with meat, whites with fish and poultry, and champagne when there's an occasion to celebrate. Even winery tours sometimes fail to advance one's viniculture education, especially if it's a warm day and every sip starts to taste the same!

There are also those who embrace the belief that the higher the price tag, the better the wine is going to be. In other words, they are buying the "prestige" with great expectation of a satisfying experience.

Not always the case, unfortunately.

Christina and I attended many a fundraising dinner wherein politicians on an expense account immediately snatched up the wine list and sought out the priciest bottle as a way to impress their guests. (I call this "reading from the right" instead of the left.) One evening in New Orleans we particularly remember was a Senator who not only pounced on a $1,200 label he knew nothing about but then proceeded to grandiosely order a second one as well.

I completely credit my own knowledge of wine to the sommeliers of some of our favorite restaurants, most especially Spago in Beverly Hills and Hélène Darroze in Paris. That they thoughtfully take the time to make suggestions has immeasurably added to my understanding of what successfully pairs with what. Further, on the occasions when my main own course has been beef and Christina's has been shrimp, they have assisted in navigating the list and identifying a single bottle which would complement both entrees without having to order separate glasses.

If all of this is new territory for you, let's start with some basics.

Red wines and white wines are categorized as being full-bodied or light-bodied.

A nicely chilled, light-bodied white wine is going to conjure thoughts of lazy summer nights and al fresco dining. These wines come from regions with cool climates and include such names as Sauvignon Blanc and Pinot Grigio.

A full-bodied white wine comes from warmer climates such as those found in Italy, Spain and California. Often aged in oak barrels to give them a smoother taste, these would include Chardonnay and Viognier.

If you prefer white wine with a sweeter taste, you may want to try a Riesling, Gewürztraminer or a Moscato. The first thing to hit your nose will be their fruity, perfumed aroma.

Light-bodied red wines are pale in color and have less headache-inducing tannins than their full-bodied counterparts. Most popular are Gamay Beaujolais and Pinot Noir. (Tannins are the chemical compounds which give wines their texture, balance and structure.)

Moving to medium-bodied red wines, we'll find Merlot, Zinfandel, Sangiovese and Barbera. Any of these match well with a wide variety of foods but especially Italian.

Want to go for something bold? Full-bodied red wines are the darkest and have the most tannins to cleanse one's palate. Cabernet Sauvignon, Malbec, Shiraz and South African Pinotage are front-runners in this category.

Looking for something in-between? Rosé wines have been around since the late 18th century but seemed to hit their stride in America in the mid-20th. They derive from red wine grapes and include White Zinfandel, Grenache and Syrah.

Want some sparkles in your life? Nothing says it better than Champagne, so named for the region in France it originally hails from. Our own favorites in this department are Prosecco, Cava and Crémant, all of which are charmingly affordable.

Dessert wines are in a class all by themselves and include Tawny and Ruby Port, Sauterne, Sherry, Madeira and Moscatel. Can an amusing cheese plate or something in chocolate be far behind?

SIMPLE PAIRINGS

If you intend to make wine a lifelong study, there's certainly nothing wrong with that. The average person, though, tends to look for (1) a wine that can be enjoyed on its own and (2) a wine which doesn't cancel out all the flavors of the meal it is supposed to accompany.

In a whimsical way, think of wine/food pairings as dance partners. For the dance to be enjoyable, they need to bring compatible skill sets. If one of them, for instance, is very large and flashy, it will be hard for anyone to take notice of a petite partner who is quietly understated. A proper balance needs to take into consideration the respective "weight" of the participants; i.e., a robust red wine would completely obliterate the delicacy of a lightly seasoned white fish.

Likewise, attention needs to be paid to whatever is the most prominent component of the entrée. In most cases, this will be the cooking method (baking, poaching, grilling, frying), the seasonings introduced and whether there is a sauce. While you might assume, for example, that a chicken dish always has to be served with white wine, consider how many different herbs and sauces can change its core personality (tomato sauce, mushroom sauce, lemon sauce, teriyaki, barbecue).

How spicy is the food you're serving? Why invite it to collide with all the tannins in a wine with high alcohol content when it could be better balanced with a lighter wine which brings complementary sweetness?

If you're new to all of this navigation, the following cheat-sheet is a smart starting point.

Vegetable Dishes and White Fish = Pinot Grigio

Seafood = Chardonnay

Chicken, Shrimp and Salads = Sauvignon Blanc

Asian Dishes and Salty Seafoods = Riesling

Pork = Sémillon

Cream-based Dishes = Pinot Grigio

Spicy Dishes = Gewürztraminer

Salty Dishes = Sparkling Wine

Honey Glazed Ham = Viognier

Steaks and Beef Stews = Cabernet Sauvignon

Grilled Meats = Shiraz

Lamb = Malbec

Tomato-based Pastas = Tempranillo

Lean Poultry = Merlot

Fatty Fish = Pinot Noir

Meat-Sauce Pastas = Chianti

Mushroom Risotto = Syrah

Smoked Ham = Sangiovese

Japanese Food = Beaujolais

Turkey = Rioja

Lastly, keep in mind that wines with high acidity are a good match for rich, savory dishes; sweet wines will balance out salty and spicy foods; and the tannins in full-bodied red wines will soften in the presence of fats and proteins.

CHRISTINA'S WINE LABEL THEORY

I've always loved going wine shopping with my wife. Although she doesn't mind gravitating to wine we have previously enjoyed, her method of picking new labels is amazingly accurate.

The operative word here is *labels*.

As someone who worked in all aspects of media, she is discerning when it comes to colors, themes, graphics and fonts. Her belief is that if a winery can afford to invest in an eye-catching and appealing label for its product, the product itself must be pretty good. Time and again she has surprised me with wines which sport a whimsical image, an Art Deco composition, bold color combinations, clever wordplay or hints of fantasy, romance and magic.

And every single time, her choices have never failed to amuse and delight.

ABOUT THE AUTHOR

Attorney. Lobbyist. Consultant. Opera singer. Savvy gourmet chef. Excellent wordsmith, proofreader and brain-stormer. Multi-lingual. Romantic and supportive husband. Devoted pet parent.

Gone from us too soon.

Mark Edward Webb

1956-2023

ABOUT THE EDITOR

Former actress and theatre director Christina Hamlett is an award-winning novelist and playwright whose credits to date include 50 books, 275 stage plays and squillions of articles and interviews. Her latest release, *Everything I Know About Widowhood I Learned From Jessica Fletcher*, is available on Amazon in paperback and Kindle. Learn more at www.authorhamlett.com[1]

If you enjoyed *The Open Door Gourmet*, you are encouraged to write a review and to share pictures of your culinary efforts on Facebook.

All proceeds from the sale of this book will go to cancer research.

---

1. http://www.authorhamlett.com

www.ingramcontent.com/pod-product-compliance
Lightning Source LLC
Chambersburg PA
CBHW021949120726
47992CB00001B/211